U·Re

Dream

universe

consciousness

c - Rex

Truth

consciousness

universe

JED MCKENNA'S
THEORY OF EVERYTHING
THE ENLIGHTENED PERSPECTIVE

Also by Jed McKenna

THE ENLIGHTENMENT TRILOGY
The trilogy is recommended, but not needed, to enjoy this book.

SPIRITUAL ENLIGHTENMENT
THE DAMNEDEST THING

SPIRITUALLY INCORRECT ENLIGHTENMENT

SPIRITUAL WARFARE

WWW.WISEFOOLPRESS.COM

Jed McKenna's Theory of Everything
The Enlightened Perspective

Print ISBN: 978-0-9891759-0-6
E-Book ISBN: 978-0-9891759-1-3
AudioBook ISBN: 978-0-9891759-2-0

Contents

Sapere Aude

Dare to Know

Horace

I do not expect any popular approval, or indeed any wide audience. On the contrary I would not urge anyone to read this book except those who are able and willing to meditate seriously with me, and to withdraw their minds from the senses and from all preconceived opinions. Such readers, as I well know, are few and far between. Those who do not bother to grasp the proper order of my arguments and the connection between them, but merely try to carp at individual sentences, as is the fashion, will not get much benefit from reading this book. They may well find an opportunity to quibble in many places, but it will not be easy for them to produce objections which are telling or worth replying to.

René Descartes

That Which Cannot Be Simpler

SOCRATES: I want to hear from him what is the nature of his art, and what it is which he professes and teaches; he may, as you suggest, defer the exhibition to some other time.

CALLICLES: There is nothing like asking him, Socrates; and indeed to answer questions is a part of his exhibition, for he was saying only just now, that any one in my house might put any question to him, and that he would answer.

SOCRATES: How fortunate! Will you ask him, Chaerephon–?

CHAEREPHON: What shall I ask him?

SOCRATES: Ask him who he is.

T HE FIRST AND LAST CHAPTERS of the trilogy were titled *That Which Cannot Be Simpler.* In the books we saw how that applied to the awakening process. Now we can take a look and see if that doesn't apply to deciphering reality as well.

"You're saying it does, I suppose?" says Karl.

"Yes, that's what I'm saying, and if I'm right about how simple it is, there should be no trouble at all in showing it to you, so that in theory, you understand it as well as I do."

"In theory?"

"Yes, what for me is a living reality, my paradigm-of-residence, can only be theory for anyone who hasn't made the actual journey. Short of that, we can certainly look together and see if it's not only very simple, but that which cannot be simplified further."

"How long do you think this will take?"

"We're unlocking all the mysteries of creation, you can't find some room in your schedule?"

"But if you're saying it's so simple…"

"Fine. Under five minutes if you play fair, seven if you obstruct."

"Why should I obstruct?"

"Maya."

"The dog?"

"The other one."

"Okay, it's two forty-seven right now. Loser buys the beer. *Good* beer."

"You're on. Do you believe that truth exists?"

"I won't make it that easy for you."

"Good, let's try it the other way. Do you believe that truth does not exist?"

"I sense a trap."

"If we say that truth does not exist, then we are saying it is true that truth does not exist; a self-nullifying statement like saying there are no absolutes. Would you agree?"

"I suppose so."

"This much is not belief or feeling, it's simple logic. Do

you find fault with the logic?"

"No, I agree that the statement *truth does not exist* is a logical contradiction."

"Therefore?"

"Based on the fact that truth cannot *not* exist, because it would be absurd to say that *no-truth is truth* is true, I agree that truth must exist. I don't know what truth is, only that something must be true."

"So you agree that something must be true. Regardless of what it might be, truth must exist. Yes?"

"Yes, I agree with that."

"I don't want to have to revisit this point because we left too soon. Do you have any reservations about agreeing that regardless of all else, something must be true?"

"I am convinced of it. No-truth can't be true, so something must be true. Four minutes left."

"Okay, now that we have determined that something must be true, regardless of what it might be, let's see what else we can say. For instance, do you think it would be possible for truth to change? Could it be one thing now and another thing later?"

"If it changes it can't possibly be true. Truth must be unchanging. Even if time comes to an end, truth must still be true or it never was."

"Okay then, even if truth is constant beyond time, could it be one thing and not another?"

"Please provide an example."

"Do you think truth could be something like light or love or beauty?"

"It doesn't seem so. Those seem to be parts of something larger and cannot really exist in their own right. They need their opposites. What is light without dark? What is good

3

without evil or love without hate? Obviously, truth cannot be a thing apart."

"So you would agree that, whatever truth is, it must be both unchanging and whole?"

"Certainly it must be constant and unchanging, yes. And I would agree it must be a whole, not a part, because what would the other part be? A different truth? Obviously not. Untruth? Obviously not."

"Well then, do you think truth could be a matter of perspective? Do you think my truth could be different from your truth? Can truth be relative?"

"Certainly not. We have established that truth must be universally true or it is not true at all."

"Would you suppose truth to be finite or infinite?"

"We have established that truth cannot be finite. If there were something else besides truth, then that thing would also have to be true, in which case neither thing could be true and the actual truth would have to be some larger, all-encompassing thing. Three minutes left."

"Patience, the one true theory of everything might take six minutes."

"Then I will receive illumination *and* beer. Am I obstructing?"

"You're being fair, but don't be too fair. Please don't let us pass any point on which you are still undecided. If I might summarize, we have so far determined that truth exists, yes?"

"That much is certain."

"And we have determined that truth cannot change; it cannot be one thing now and another thing later. It has to be unchanging. Is that right?"

"Yes, I agree that truth must be unchanging or else it's no

more true than the chirp of a bird or the shape of a cloud."

"And yet, is it not possible that whatever we discover truth to be, it must prove to be found in all things? That nothing that exists can be exempt from truth, or exist outside of truth?"

"Very possible. In fact, I must insist on it. Truth must be found in the essential nature of all that exists, and nothing can exist independently of truth. It's absurd to suggest that something might exist in untruth."

"And we have determined that truth cannot be a part of something larger, or half of a whole. Are we agreed on this?"

"I agree that truth cannot be limited or finite. I freely stipulate that it must be universal and unlimited, without boundaries."

"So truth must be infinite?"

"It must be so."

"Truth is absolute then, not part or subset or aspect?"

"Certainly. Truth must be absolute or it is not truth at all. It's two fifty. Two minutes left."

"Just to be clear, can there be two truths?"

"Definitively not! If one thing is absolutely true, another thing cannot also be absolutely true. If the other thing is absolutely true, then the first thing could not have been. It's very simple."

"Thank you. Would you say then that truth exists within time and space?"

"Well, it would be absurd to think so. That would make it finite and changing, but if truth is finite and changing then it's not absolute. Therefore, truth does not exist within time and space which are both changing and impermanent."

"So Captain Ahab was correct, in your opinion, when he

said truth hath no confines?"

"It must be so, for if truth has confines, what is beyond those confines? More truth? Truth must be infinite."

"And what of untruth? Where does that fit in?"

"It doesn't. There can plainly be no such thing as untruth. I don't pretend to understand it, and I cannot make it fit reality as I see it, but the logic is perfectly sound. It is beyond question that truth is absolute and that untruth does not exist. Untruth cannot be *true* any more than non-being can *be* or non-existence can *exist*."

"Then, to summarize again, you agree that truth exists, and you would further say that untruth does not exist. Have we left any single point unresolved in your thinking?"

"No, just in sitting here for the last few minutes I see that because truth must be absolute, the matter is quite plain. Truth must exist and untruth cannot exist. The clock is ticking. Two fifty-one. One minute left. I fear for you."

"Well, I'm sorry to disappoint you, but it seems I have gone too quickly. I would take a moment now to light a cigarette and put my feet up, but I don't smoke and my feet are already up."

"Tick-tock. Fifty seconds."

"But we're practically done. We've determined that truth exists and must be absolute. What could be simpler? We've stated the first premise of an airtight syllogism: Truth is all. Do you disagree?"

"The matter is beyond rational dispute. Truth exists and untruth is not possible, so truth is all. There is only truth. It cannot be otherwise. I agree entirely."

"So now, to determine what truth is, we need only determine what, with absolute certainty, exists. What can you say, with absolute certainty, that is true?"

"Easy, philosophy 101. I can say I Am. I know that I exist. Fifteen seconds."

"And what is the nature of your existence?"

"The nature of my existence? Consciousness, of course. I am conscious and your time is up. I find this all very interesting and I would like to continue our conversation, but you owe me a beer. A *good* beer."

"I would like to continue this conversation too, as we drink the beer *you* will provide because we have just solved every single mystery in existence in five minutes."

"Did we? Then why do I still not know?"

"You do, you just haven't realized it yet, which I don't think should count against my five minutes, do you?"

"Not if it is as you say, but I don't see that you have done what you claim."

"Are you familiar with syllogisms?"

"Yes, logic; if/and/then. *If* all men are mortal *and* Socrates is a man, *then* Socrates is mortal."

"Yes, that's the famous one. Two premises; all men are mortal and Socrates is a man, prove a proposition; Socrates is mortal. If the premises are true, the proposition must be true."

"And we created a syllogism in your five minutes?"

"We did. A stable, airtight, perfect syllogistic proof. We determined that truth is all and that consciousness exists, both as certainties, did we not?"

"Truth is all, yes. And to say I exist is the same as to say consciousness exists, yes."

"Can you say that anything else exists?"

"No. I am quite familiar with the cogito and solipsism and your books, and I have determined this to my complete satisfaction. The only thing I know for certain is that I exist, which is the same as saying that consciousness exists."

"And if we were to state these points syllogistically?"

"Truth is all and consciousness exists? I guess we would say *if* truth is all, *and* consciousness exists, *then*... ahhh, *then I owe you a beer.*"

"A *good* beer."

✧

That which cannot be simpler:

if	Truth is All
and	Consciousness Exists
then	Consciousness is All

Here We Go Again

Sometimes I sits and thinks,
and sometimes I just sits.

Satchel Paige

I MEMORIZED THE DAYS OF THE WEEK back when that was all the rage, but these days I only think in terms of two kinds of days; normal days and people-aren't-doing-their-job days. It was a people-aren't-doing-their-job day, and I, as always, was doing my job. On this day, my job involved swinging in a hammock with my hat pulled down which, for all my talk about it, was something I'd never actually done.

✣

That's how this chapter originally began, and how it still does, I suppose. The original version went on way too much without actually saying much, so I pared it back to not so much, as follows:

Maya and I were visiting an area where I once owned a small piece of land that no one else knew about. The main feature of this wooded, hilly place was an old, overgrown rock-and-mortar foundation next to a creek. I think it had once been a church, so that's how I thought of it. Over time, I tended and groomed the shallow foundations. I rerouted the stream so the water flowed into the small higher section, then poured over a rock ledge into the large lower section, creating a pair of tranquil ponds. The lowest opening in the low section fed out to three wide stone steps, so the water flowed down over those and through a me-made channel back into the stream. I enjoyed puttering around and arranging it, and used it as my private place for several years. It was a useless and unsalable property, so when I left the area I offered it to an acquaintance, Karl, hoping he would take a liking to it and enjoy it with his wife Sandy and their growing twins. He accepted. That was years ago.

On this trip, I wanted to revisit the place, so Maya and I drove out to the state park from which my former happy place was accessed. I expected the place to have completely returned to nature like I originally found it almost two decades earlier, but instead I found it much nicer than I left it. I didn't expect to meet up with anyone, but it was a people-aren't-doing-their-jobs day and it turns out that Karl and family visit for a picnic on the occasional weekend. So, as is often the case, what I hoped wouldn't happen happened, and turned out to be very fortuitous.

❖

Several nights before this nostalgic Sunday outing, I was lying in a hotel room with Maya. We were half-watching a science program and half-dozing, when something happened that hadn't happened in years, and which I was pretty sure would never happen again.

Science ambassador Michio Kaku was talking about the Higgs boson and the Large Hadron Collider and about how science hoped to reduce the big messy Standard Model down to an elegant little theory of everything, when, with a nudge from Maya, the words *theory of everything* spiked in my brain. It's their term, science's, coined by a physicist, but it's so grandiose and, frankly, so beyond the realm of science, that hearing it in my half-awake state triggered something in me that felt like a new writing project. I was not expecting that.

A little backstory. A few decades earlier I made a journey that very few make, and I wrote three books about it. As it happens, one of the things you get when you make this particular journey is perfect knowledge; complete and absolute understanding of everything. I never really explained that part before, but I guess I'm explaining it now.

So, I heard Dr. Kaku talk about a theory of everything, and though I'd certainly heard it before, this time it set something off in me. Obviously, I know, science doesn't and can't have a theory of everything. Equally obviously, I *must* have one. I mean, either I have a theory of everything that's not a theory, and does cover everything, and is true and unimpeachable, or else I am totally full of shit and always have been. That would be a damn interesting turn of events, but not terribly likely. I mention it because it's something you should be wondering. Anyone who says they're truth-realized or enlightened should be able to come up with an airtight, no-belief-required explanation of absolutely everything. It shouldn't be too hard, there's only one.

Then it occurred to me that, yes, of course I have a theory of everything, but no, I'd never really shared it. Now, for the first time, that seemed a little weird. Now, for the first time, it seemed like something I should express. So now, for the first time since wrapping up the trilogy project, it seemed like there was something else that needed saying.

✧

"That's all you have?" asks Karl, shuffling through a small stack of printed pages.

"I just started," I reply.

"What about the original version you mention?"

"That was around thirty pages of longhand, already up in flames."

"I'll bet it was nice," he says, "all about how we found you at the ponds, so lonely and sad, and we took you in and put a roof over your head, and encouraged you to write again, and taught you to drink good beer."

"It sounds different when you say it," I say. Actually, everything sounds different when Karl says it. English is his fourth or fifth language, and he has a unique accent. He is chronically cheerful and strangely large, as if he's a smaller sample of some bigger, happier species.

We're sitting in the outdoor livingroom in Karl's backyard. Maya and I are guests in his detached in-law apartment and have been here for a few days now.

"You are writing about a theory of everything," Karl asks in a tone that doesn't need a question mark.

"Not just *a* theory," I say, "the only possible theory of everything is truth. That's pretty obvious, isn't it? I mean, what can we know as truth? The cogito, right? Only the fact that I exist; I Am."

"Yes, I understand this."

"Then what can science know as truth?'

"Nothing more than this, I think."

"Yeah, right. I Am is the fundamental universal constant of knowledge. Everything else is belief. The speed of light is not a true constant, but the knowledge constant is."

"Why do you say the speed of light is not constant?"

"Because time, space and light don't exist."

He stares at me for a moment as if waiting for the punchline.

"That sounds quite insane," he says.

"It sure does," I agree, and think of the Sherlock Holmes quote we used in one of the books: *When you have eliminated all which is impossible, then whatever remains, however improbable, must be the truth.*

✧

So now I'm swinging in the hammock in Karl's backyard, writing notes about, of all things, a theory of everything. That's what I get for watching science shows at bedtime. Of course, I'm not a scientist or a philosopher, or a religious or spiritual thinker, or even very bright or motivated for that matter. What I am is truth-realized, so if you read the trilogy and you're with me this far, then you have my credentials as tour guide – but you also know you don't need them. As always, you need only look for yourself.

And if you haven't read the trilogy, no worries. This theory of everything stuff stands on its own.

I shouldn't call it *a* theory of everything. It's not. It's *theee* theory of everything, and it's really not a theory at all. It has no theoretical element. It's directly knowable as clear and obvious truth to people with even regular sized brains, and to see it for ourselves, we just have to stop seeing mystery where there is none.

"So, for you there is no more mystery?" asks Karl.

"No," I reply, "if there were more mystery I wouldn't have been done when I was done. There would have still been further. As I hope I made clear in the books, done means done. It's the end of the line, the end of questions, the end of knowledge."

"I know this from your books," he says, "but it's hard to believe there is such a thing."

Karl and Sandy invited me to stay in their in-law apartment over their garage for as long as I would like. It's been converted into a music studio, but it's still a very comfortable living space. In their backyard is a covered outdoor living area with couches, tables, lamps, ceiling fans and a hammock. They have a nice black lab named Duke who seems sweet on Maya, my Border Collie, but in the sense that I'm a dog person, Maya isn't a dog dog. She doesn't dislike other dogs, she just doesn't see any point in them. She'll sniff a butt now and then, but she's not that into it. Anyway, Karl's guesthouse is a nice place for me to work, and Maya likes it, so we accepted their invitation to hang out for awhile.

I sway in the hammock and play with ideas and doze and throw toys for Maya and jot things down as I think of them. I fill about ten pages with loosely scrawled notes until I feel spent, then I drift off and let my mind breathe. Then, refreshed, I boil my scribbled notes down to this jumbled mess:

consciousness is primary/comes 1st ... prior to time, space, matter, duality, causality etc ... all within/nothing without ...

nothing prior to c ... c=p³, one true model of reality, answer to everything ... bulletproof, unassailable, anomaly-free, perfect, flawless .... alpha/omega science/philosophy/spirituality/religion ... end search/quest/mystery ... explains everything, leaves nothing unexplained ... kills every buddha ... no entity can say more ... clear & simple, available to direct knowing ... theory of everything ... truth entire ... pasupatastra, the thought that destroys etc ... consciousness is king ... c-prime ... con-rex ...

I set my notes aside and wonder why I'm thinking about all this. Am I doing this because I want to understand it better? Did the science program trigger something in me? It's now more than five years since I've done any writing, more than six since that final click that marked the end of the trilogy for me, and I haven't missed it – much. A little, sure. It's nice to have a larger-than-self project, to collaborate, to express well and to bring that expression to completion and conclusion. I enjoyed being engaged by the trilogy project for the six or seven years I was involved with it, but when it was over, I saw and understood its overness. I was satisfied that it was complete and have not felt any urge to write more since that happy click.

The process I underwent, the time I spent communicating, the books, none of that has much presence in my life. I make this point because I think some folks might assume that once you become what I've become, that it becomes your full-time thing, but for me it's just a minor oddity from my past. I might go days at a time without thinking about it at all, and when I do, it feels like a dream fragment, like a memory I can't fully trust. Did I really do all that stuff and write those books? Yeah, I guess so. Wow, that's pretty weird.

My main reminder is that I inhabit a different paradigm from everyone around me, but there aren't that many people around me, so it doesn't come up much. Even when it does, it's my new normal and lost its novelty long ago.

✧

Actually, I have considered writing a book on the subject of energetic flow and alignment, smooth effortless functioning and all that. I've seen that there are many books about manifesting desires, prayer and conscious creation, using this or that technique to achieve this or that outcome, and I have wondered if it might be a subject on which I could make a contribution.

But no. All of this was covered in the trilogy as well as I can cover it. The key is Human Adulthood, and my sense is that most of the books out there are unclear on this, so they are, in effect, teaching Human Children how to make the most of childhood rather than outgrow it. I wouldn't have any interest, or receive any co-creative participation, in teaching Human Children how to do anything except become Human Adults, and then continuing in that direction of development. Human Adulthood is the key that unlocks life, and I can't think of anything I might add to what was said in the books.

✧

So now, five years later, I'm surprised to find that my writer sense is tingling again. Or is it? That question actually answers itself. If I'm not sure, then it's not. I'm not going to embark on a new writing project for any other reason than because I receive clear instruction to do so, and if I'm not sure I have, then I haven't. I don't write for my own purposes anymore, as I did with Spiritual Autolysis, so the only reason I would write is because, as described in *Warfare*, I receive a clear understanding and the support is in place, so that, in effect, it's not me writing, but a co-creative process in which I play a role and everyone knows their part. I don't push or pull or steer. I wait for the pieces to appear and then proceed into effortless clarity. That's not just for writing, that's for everything. I relax into the larger process. I allow unfolding and flow with subtle currents.

Of course, you know that this project eventually got greenlighted, but at this early note-taking stage I didn't think it would. I thought my trip was making me nostalgic, or that I was just a little bored.

This Thing You're Reading

I didn't have time to write a short letter,
so I wrote a long one instead.

Mark Twain

I TOOK THE TIME TO WRITE a short document. I wrote the first draft in about three weeks while staying at Karl's, then I filled it out in about two months, then I took another two months to cut it in half and then another two months to cut it in half again. I could have let it go four months earlier and four times longer, but this material isn't wide-ranging like the trilogy; it's really just one thing viewed from many angles. It has all the inherent complexity of any attempt at cross-paradigm communication, but it doesn't benefit from overtelling. Less is definitely more.

One problem with this theory-of-everything project is that I never had to reduce my new worldview down to words before, and it's a pretty weird thing to do. This is not a minor issue. This is paradigm-level stuff and virtually everyone, regardless of other differences, inhabits the same top-level paradigm. How would you describe your reality to someone from another? Can you even think of a story or film that takes place in a different top-level paradigm? I've wracked my brain for many long seconds without success.

The paradigm gap between reader and writer is real and wide. I'm expressing theory, but I'm not operating from theory. I'm decompiling the enlightened perspective for the purpose of expression, but this is my living reality. I suppose it's to be expected that any paradigm other than one's own must necessarily seem insane, but if that's where truth leads, then that's where seekers gotta go.

After a minute of exhaustive research, I discovered that paradigm is another term we are borrowing from science and putting to better use. In scientific terms, if you change your set of assumptions about the universe from Newtonian to Einsteinian, you have made a paradigm shift. In this document, I use paradigm to mean worldview in the broadest possible sense. Because everyone shares the same top-level paradigm – time and space, energy and matter, duality and causality, etc – no one ever has to reduce it to words. Everyone gets it. We're all on the same page.

So, my two issues in writing this are, one, reducing the living reality of an unknown paradigm – mine – down to very inadequate words, and two, transmitting an understanding of my unknown paradigm with these very inadequate words into a completely different paradigm, one I once inhabited but which is now completely unreal to me – yours.

I am suited to the task I performed in becoming the person who could write the trilogy, but I have no personal ambition to do more. I'm making a reasonable effort with this theory-of-everything stuff, but it's really an afterthought. This is probably a good time to mention that I am not a spiritual person and never was, and that, in my view, the search for truth is not a spiritual endeavor and never was. What's more, the truth is that truth is not really relevant. It has no practical value or realworld application. It doesn't change or improve anything. I may understand that consensus reality isn't true, or even probable, but here I am. Truth is outside of all paradigms, but we live inside them.

Just as I wouldn't want to overstate my qualifications, nor would I want to understate them. I reside in the one and only not-false paradigm. I see what is and I don't see what's not, so I don't need belief to hide some parts or fill in others. Nevertheless, I am retired. I don't think anymore because thinking is the only real weapon of mass destruction, and I don't need it anymore. I have thought the universe to death.

As far as enlightenment goes, I am a perfect master. My truth-realization is absolute. I can have equals but not superiors. As far as communicating goes, I do a pretty fair job, but I am not a master communicator. Now, entering into this current subject, I am not a master of anything, I just have a clear view. I have no mind for science and philosophy or theology – that stuff bores me numb – so make allowances for this. What I am saying here is not for you to trust or believe, but to look into on your own.

In all but the broadest sense, none of this makes much sense. I am supposedly enlightened, and I am writing for you, the reader, a document explaining that you and I don't exist, and that the world in which we don't exist – in which

I am transmitting and you are receiving – also doesn't exist. Kind of.

But in the broadest sense it all makes perfect sense, and this document is all about the broadest sense. A theory of everything can't be anything less than the view from the highest altitude, and must therefore be both true *and* the enlightened perspective.

The King of Pointland

Excerpted from Flatland, a Romance of Many
Dimensions, *by Edwin Abbott Abbott, 1884. The
two-dimensional narrator is being introduced to a
broader reality by a three-dimensional sphere. They
visit scorn upon a dimensionless point that is content and
unshakable in its certainty that it is the totality of being.
Is the dimensionless point all or nothing? Wise or fool?*

"LOOK YONDER," SAID MY GUIDE, "in Flatland thou hast
lived; of Lineland thou hast received a vision; thou
hast soared with me to the heights of Spaceland; now, in
order to complete the range of thy experience, I conduct thee
downward to the lowest depth of existence, even to the realm
of Pointland, the Abyss of No dimensions.

"Behold yon miserable creature. That Point is a Being like ourselves, but confined to the non-dimensional Gulf. He is himself his own World, his own Universe; of any other than himself he can form no conception; he knows not Length, nor Breadth, nor Height, for he has had no experience of them; he has no cognizance even of the number Two; nor has he a thought of Plurality; for he is himself his One and All, being really Nothing. Yet mark his perfect self-contentment, and hence learn this lesson, that to be self-contented is to be vile and ignorant, and that to aspire is better than to be blindly and impotently happy. Now listen."

He ceased; and there arose from the little buzzing creature a tiny, low, monotonous, but distinct tinkling, as from one of your Spaceland phonographs, from which I caught these words, "Infinite beatitude of existence! It is; and there is none else beside It."

"What," said I, "does the puny creature mean by 'it'?"

"He means himself," said the Sphere: "have you not noticed before now, that babies and babyish people who cannot distinguish themselves from the world, speak of themselves in the Third Person? But hush!"

"It fills all Space," continued the little soliloquizing Creature, "and what It fills, It is. What It thinks, that It utters; and what It utters, that It hears; and It itself is Thinker, Utterer, Hearer, Thought, Word, Audition; it is the One, and yet the All in All. Ah, the happiness ah, the happiness of Being!"

"Can you not startle the little thing out of its complacency?" said I. "Tell it what it really is, as you told me; reveal to it the narrow limitations of Pointland, and lead it up to something higher."

"That is no easy task," said my Master; "try you."

Hereon, raising my voice to the uttermost, I addressed the Point as follows:

"Silence, silence, contemptible Creature. You call yourself the All in All, but you are the Nothing: your so-called Universe is a mere speck in a Line, and a Line is a mere shadow as compared with—"

"Hush, hush, you have said enough," interrupted the Sphere, "now listen, and mark the effect of your harangue on the King of Pointland."

The lustre of the Monarch, who beamed more brightly than ever upon hearing my words, shewed clearly that he retained his complacency; and I had hardly ceased when he took up his strain again. "Ah, the joy, ah, the joy of Thought! What can It not achieve by thinking! Its own Thought coming to Itself, suggestive of Its disparagement, thereby to enhance Its happiness! Sweet rebellion stirred up to result in triumph! Ah, the divine creative power of the All in One! Ah, the joy, the joy of Being!"

"You see," said my Teacher, "how little your words have done. So far as the Monarch understands them at all, he accepts them as his own – for he cannot conceive of any other except himself – and plumes himself upon the variety of 'Its Thought' as an instance of creative Power. Let us leave this God of Pointland to the ignorant fruition of his omnipresence and omniscience: nothing that you or I can do can rescue him from his self-satisfaction."

Hammocky Ponderings

It is in the infinite ocean of myself that the
mind-creation called the world takes place.

Ashtavakra Gita

S TILL IN THE HAMMOCK, I read my notes and try to boil it
down a bit. After a few minutes I have this:

*consciousness/superset/universe ... universe/subset/
consciousness ... i-am/consciousness = truth ... all else = belief
... time, space & duality = belief ... energy, matter & causality =
belief ... life, death & god = belief ... no belief is true ... untruth
does not exist ... there is only truth
... consciousness is king ... c-rex ...*

I stare at my notes for several minutes and sigh. It looks
like I have a writing project on my hands.

✧

"C-Rex?" asks Karl.

"Yeah, C-Rex, consciousness is king, as opposed to U-Rex, universe is king, which is the reigning paradigm we all know and love."

Karl reads through my notes. He takes his time.

"No," he says, "I don't think so."

We discuss it for a few minutes.

"The difference between U-Rex and C-Rex is simple," I explain to him. "Imagine a sheet of white paper and put a dot somewhere in the middle of it. The white page is infinite, it goes on forever in all directions. Okay?'

"Yes, okay."

"Now, label the infinite sheet of paper Universe, and label the dot Consciousness. Okay?"

"Okay."

"That's what I'm calling U-Rex, our shared paradigm of reality. Regardless of any other consideration, that's how everyone understands their reality. I am conscious, and my consciousness is one small thing in a great big universe. Agree?"

"Certainly," he says.

"And that universe is just as we know it. It has time and space, energy and matter, everything we all experience all the time. It's full of people and planets and stars, incomprehensible vastness and complexity, everything we mean by universe, right?"

"Fine, yes."

"That's the reigning paradigm of reality. Universe is king, U-Rex. Your consciousness is a dot, one small thing in an infinite universe."

"Yes."

"Got that piece of paper in mind?"

"Yes." He smiles indulgently, but his eyes are bright with intelligence. "So how do we arrive at this other paradigm of yours?"

"Just switch the labels."

The smile stays on his face but I can see that his thoughts have turned inward. He stays that way for many long seconds.

"No," he says through his smile, "I don't think so."

✢

Oh yeah, definitely. C-Rex: Consciousness is King. Consciousness is the superset of the universe, not the other way around or any other way. Once we make that one minor adjustment in our thinking, reality resolves into perfect clarity. Every question is answered/destroyed. Every mystery is solved/nullified. Nothing is left unexplained, no violation of reason occurs. Recompiling reality based on this new perspective might take years, but as far as the theory of everything goes, that's it. C-Rex, Consciousness is King; the one true, comprehensive, bulletproof, fireproof, idiotproof, geniusproof theory of everything.

✢

"Okay, wait a minute," says Karl. "Do you know what you're saying? You make it sound very easy, like yes, you just switch labels, but do you know that if you do that... what that means? I mean, do you even know what that would mean?"

"I think I do," I say.

"That would mean there is no universe," he says with a bit of an edge, "that we're just imagining the whole thing."

"Something like that, yes."

"You're saying there is no actual universe?"

"I'm saying there is no actual anything."

✧

That evening, at Karl's request, I briefly explain C-Rex to the others as we sit around the sparkling flames of the tabletop gas fire. Sandy is knitting while we talk. Her mother, Grams, came for dinner and sits beside her with a glass of wine. I was warned that I probably wouldn't like Grams, but I'm not a big people person, so I figured not liking one more wouldn't be a problem.

"Is there really a single theory of everything?" asks Claire, Karl and Sandy's college-age daughter.

"One answer that explains everything?" asks John, Claire's twin brother.

"Certainly," I reply, "truth. Truth is the one answer, of course; the only possible theory of everything."

"But what is truth?" asks John.

"That's the big question," adds Claire.

"Yeah," confirms John.

"Truth is absolute," I say, "unchanging and attributeless, one without other, beyond time and space. Encompassing all and encompassed by nothing. Whatever meets those criteria must be true."

"And you're saying it's consciousness?" says Claire.

I give them the short version about switching the labels and they discuss it with their father for a few minutes while I work on my notes. Finally, Grams delivers the verdict.

"What a load of crap," she says, and I'm surprised to find out that I do like her. She's exactly right. It *is* a load of crap. It's the most unbelievable nonsense you could possibly make up, and except for the fact that it's true, and except for the fact that it's my home paradigm, I would think it every bit as ridiculous as this no-nonsense old lady thinks it.

✧

"We got a Zen coin for you," proudly announced John when we were introduced years earlier.

"What's the sound of one hand clapping?" Claire presented the koan. They were eight or nine at the time.

"I don't know," I replied, "what's the sound of *two* hands clapping?"

They squealed in delight and clapped their hands to answer my question, but the question remains unanswered. We don't have to be so clever about our questions that we leave our assumptions unmolested. What's the sound of two hands clapping? That's all the Zen coin anyone needs. Get to the bottom of *any*thing and you'll get to the bottom of *every*thing. Just pick a spot and start digging.

✧

"So you were watching TV, minding your own business, and suddenly you conceived a theory of everything?" Karl asks me later that evening. We're walking slow laps with Maya and his dog Duke in a nearby park among other people and their kids and dogs.

"Kind of," I say. "It actually never occurred to me to write about this topic until the science program about a theory of everything. That's what sparked it. My immediate thought was that the only possible theory of everything is truth, and that I live it. I know everything about it, and I may be one of very few who do, and one of even fewer who are designed for expression. Science uses the term theory of everything in a very non-everything sense, so I'm just appropriating their phrase and elevating it to its fullest rightful meaning."

"Was all this in your books?"

"It must have been since it's my worldview, my perspective. I can think of a few examples from the books, like how I couldn't distinguish between the end of the world and the snapping of a twig, how I'm one with all I see, how laughing babies and child burn wards were no different to me, that sort of thing. From the gated side it looks like non-attachment, but from this side such a term is meaningless. Any mention I made of *tat tvam asi*, that thou art, *neti neti*, nonduality, comes back to this. I think I said that, to lazier observers, the enlightened state could appear evil or psychotic. Julie said at one point in her letters that she knew the part I hadn't told, that's probably this. Any mention of the dreamstate is this, of course. I haven't gone back and looked at the books, but this worldview, C-Rex, must be reflected throughout because it's *my* worldview. This is where I live."

"Julie said you don't miss a trick."

"No trick to miss, that's right. I'm not making this stuff up, just saying what I see."

"Is there a reason you didn't say more about this in the books?"

"Several. One, I never translated all this into words before now. The only accurate description of anything is the thing itself, and anything less must fall far short. For virtually everyone, even across the greatest divides, the living reality of U-Rex is pretty much the same, so the need to describe or defend it doesn't arise. No one discovers the challenges of expression because there's no outsider to express it to. Even aliens and higher order beings would be, by our general reckoning, inhabitants of the U-Rex paradigm. But when you try to express your living worldview with someone who doesn't share it, you find it very difficult to crunch what is essentially your entire universe down into bite-size pieces. It all starts looking a little ridiculous in words, but living it isn't ridiculous at all."

Duke stays close to Karl. Maya has disappeared.

"On top of that," I continue, "it seems quite natural that no one can believe that there's a worldview other than their own. I'm somewhat unique in that I have fully inhabited two paradigms. When I was in U-Rex I would have considered the idea of C-Rex absurd and unbelievable, just as I now consider U-Rex absurd and unbelievable."

"But you actually lived in U-Rex."

"That doesn't make it true any more than last night's dream was true. I awoke from it and when I looked back I saw quite clearly that it was never there."

"So you underwent a paradigm shift?"

"Uh, well, yes and no."

✣

The term paradigm shift gets used too loosely. At the lower levels of religion, politics, science and culture, we can hop around freely, but paradigm at the highest level transcends and encompasses everything. The closest thing we have to a real paradigm shift is between dreaming and waking, but even that is not top level. The idea that the top-level paradigm we all share is false, and that another one, which we all find ridiculous, is true, isn't likely to go viral.

Karl and I walk and talk about paradigms. This isn't me instructing Karl, this is us trying to make this stuff make sense so I can make sense of it here. We walk among other evening strollers. Maya makes a brief appearance and runs off through the trees again.

"Any other paradigms you'd like to mention?" he asks.

"In the top-level sense," I say, "I can't even make up another paradigm. Maybe something where space flows in one direction and time has three dimensions or something, I don't know. We can use the term X-Rex to account for the possibility of another top-level paradigm, but I can't make one up. We'll have to leave that one for the science-fiction writers."

"It seems like there's a lot of overlap between these paradigms," says Karl, "that many elements of your C-Rex paradigm are also found in U-Rex, such as the higher functioning you talk about."

"Well, in effect, there's total overlap because we're all in consciousness. U-Rex is merely a misinterpretation of C-Rex, which is where we all are, so naturally, anyone in U-Rex can at times and to some degree avail themselves of the higher functions that come standard with C-Rex; higher knowing and navigation, non-ordinary perception, manifestation, outrageous luck, flow, observable patterns and all that. That's because those higher functions are always there, always available. You don't have to be worthy of these higher functions or know how to summon them, you just have to stop obstructing them."

Maya returns from her forays and seems very pleased with herself. She has rolled in something unspeakably disgusting, and can't wait to share it with me.

✦

"Yeah, yeah," I hear you thinking, "but what does a theory of everything do for me, right now? My situation is that I don't know shit and I'm going to die, and all this endless science and philosophy and religion and spirituality is the very muck in which I'm drowning. I don't care what the future promises. I don't care where things are headed or what the next century might hold. I don't want to be happy or radiant or blissful, I just want to stop being a schmuck. I could be dead before dinner, and I don't want to die like some baffled cow. I want to stop sleepwalking and rip my eyes open and see who and what and where I really am. I'm stuck in a quickmud coma, but I have sufficient evidence to believe that I can haul myself out. I *probably* won't, but I *possibly* can. That's a fair deal, and now I have to decide if I want to take it or just live out my days in this bovine stupor."

That's what I'd be thinking, anyway.

So what's the answer? Will this book hurtle you out of one paradigm and into another? No, definitely not. Understanding C-Rex can't do anything for you that you won't do for yourself. It won't even make you more interesting at cocktail parties. In fact, as Grams was kind enough to point out, it could get you nominated for Village Idiot, so you might want to keep it to yourself.

Chinatown

An experience is never factual but only conceptual.
Whatever an experience may be, it is nonetheless
only a happening in consciousness.

Ramesh Balsekar

IF I WANTED TO BE SUPER-ANALMAN (boy, there's a superhero costume I wouldn't want to design) (or wear), I would litter this document with asterisks tied to footnotes like this one*, followed by lengthy untanglings, but I don't like footnotes or treating readers like infants. I think you would be well advised to relax, understand the limitations of communicating at cross-paradigms, and trust yourself to decipher the message in time. Consider Descartes' words in the frontmatter and let your quibbling brain take the day off. The theory is the easy part. Recompiling personal reality over a period of years or decades is where the real work comes in.

---

* Inherent contradictions notwithstanding.

We'll see this again and again in the following pages. There might be five apparent contradictions in a single sentence. My advice; don't get caught up in the wording. Worry about the meaning, not the challenges of expression. Don't be one of Descartes' quibblers – don't settle for so little.

If we can agree to this now, it will save the tremendous amount of bloat that would be incurred by having to use three sentences to untwist every one. This stuff is really pretty simple, but there are inherent contradictions in the expression of it. This doesn't reflect on the merit of the ideas being conveyed, but on the trickiness of conveying them. Enjoy the ride and try not to think too much, you'll just end up outsmarting yourself.

✧

To describe the C-Rex paradigm requires terminology that living in it doesn't. Words are just little metaphors for meaning. I understand my paradigm directly without the need for little metaphors, so if I wish to describe it to someone who does not understand it directly, I need to make sure all my little metaphors are working for the process, not against it. If I start talking about solipsism and the cogito and the void, then I'm using little metaphors that have a built-up crust from long abuse and misuse that might make them worse than useless for our needs, and if I want to go further than our existing catalog of rusty old metaphors allows, I have to come up with some shiny new ones.

For example, I don't have a good feeling about the term theory of everything. In the same way, I never had a good feeling about the term spiritual enlightenment. They're not my terms, but in both cases I'm stuck with them because they are the established and recognized terms that provide me with a clear point of departure. Without that, I'd end up showing the wrong people the wrong stuff.

For instance, the best term I ever came up with for the truth realized state is untruth-unrealization, but if I went around calling it that and sticking it in book titles, we'd have been stopped before we started, so we went with enlightenment as an opening gambit and addressed the terminology issue within:

> Truth is absolute, there's nothing more than that, so if someone says enlightenment doesn't mean truth-realization, then it's enlightenment they're diminishing, not truth. There's nothing more than truth, and anything less than true is false, so to say that enlightenment means something other than truth-realization necessarily means you're saying it's within delusion, which doesn't sound very enlightened.

That seems clear and final to me, like simple math. In using the term enlightenment, I was equating it with the highest possible state, and there is no higher anything than truth. I don't say I'm enlightened, I say I'm truth-realized, and then point out that enlightenment must mean the same thing or be both inferior and untrue.

So, theory of everything is something we're stuck with, at least for openers.

⁜

In the U-Rex paradigm, Universe is the superset. Time, space, energy, matter, causality and duality are all subsets of the universe; parts, elements, aspects. Consciousness is also a subset of the universe; my consciousness, your consciousness, innumerable discrete consciousnesses. In short, U-Rex is reality as everyone knows it. It's so obvious and universally accepted that no one seriously doubts it. Science and mathematics are built upon it, philosophies give it the nod, and no one takes serious issue with it. Even Descartes said that no sane person doubts it.

U-Rex is reality as we know it, but when we want to speak accurately we call it Consensus Reality to remind ourselves of what is so easy to forget – that it has no basis in fact. It isn't *real* reality, it's *best-guess* reality, *let's-just-agree-and-move-on* reality. Nevertheless, U-Rex is reality as we understand it. It is the dominant and uncontested cradle-to-grave paradigm for everyone who has ever lived. Regardless of whatever differences might separate us, U-Rex is the shared paradigm of all humanity and beyond; the *universal* paradigm, it seems fair to say.

✧

In the U-Rex paradigm, universe is the superset of consciousness. C-Rex simply swaps the two, putting consciousness in the superset position. With that one minor adjustment, everything resolves into perfect clarity.

As a consequence of C-Rex, the universe as we know it ceases to exist. Absolutely. This might be the tricky part to grok; no universe, no time and space, no energy or matter, no duality or causality. All gone. Everything is inside consciousness and nothing is outside. There is no universe, there is only consciousness.

I'd like to repeat that last bit. There is only consciousness. Whatever exists is merely appearance within consciousness. There is no universe *out there*, there is no *out there* at all, there is only the universe *in here*. There is *only* consciousness. Anything that tells you otherwise is a belief, and no belief is true.

In order to recognize the truth of C-Rex, we must recognize

the untruth of U-Rex. In U-Rex, nothing makes sense, and the only thing that can ever make sense is that nothing can ever make sense. In C-Rex, everything makes perfect sense right out of the box, even the compelling apparency of the U-Rex universe. Nothing is excluded or swept under the rug, nothing is mysterious or hidden, nothing requires Einsteinian intelligence or supercolliders or space telescopes to be understood, nothing requires intermediaries or intercessors to translate for us. It's all very simple and obvious and directly knowable. How could truth be otherwise?

Not only is C-Rex comprehensive and flawless and dependent on no belief whatsoever, it's also the only possible theory of everything that can make that claim. Unlike any other model or theory of reality, C-Rex requires no belief or faith. C-Rex is what's left when belief and faith are gone. Stake life upon truth and this is where you go. There is nowhere else. There is no other truth to realize, no other enlightenment. This is where real Zen gets you. This is where asking Who am I? gets you. This is where Spiritual Autolysis gets you. This is Done.

C-Rex is the only model of reality that doesn't require belief. There is actually nothing about it to believe. In fact, stop believing everything, cancel your subscriptions, reformat your drives, cut away all that is false, burn everything, and you'll find that you never really left. C-Rex is where you've been all along.

❖

The model of reality I am calling C-Rex is simple and obvious to me. Unburdened by belief, I am able to perceive without the obscuring and distorting filters of wrong-knowing. I do not see what's not, or not see what is. Nevertheless, I am not a proponent or proselytizer for C-Rex. I'm not trying to convince anyone of anything, I'm just describing what I see, and I think that anyone who wants to understand C-Rex in theory, and is willing to relax their opposing beliefs a bit, will be able to do so.

Or, you can go the truth-realization route, and then all the C-Rex business falls into place completely on its own. C-Rex is my living reality now just as U-Rex once was, but I didn't come at it from this concept angle. I underwent a transformation as described in the trilogy, and this is where I ended up. In fact, there is nowhere else *to* end up. If you're not at C-Rex, you're not at the end.

The simple fact is that the facts are simple. Anyone of able mind should be able to theoretically comprehend the true nature of existence rather easily. Anyone who wants to transition into C-Rex as a living reality can accept the trilogy and this document as my testimony that it is an achievable and inhabitable paradigm. C-Rex isn't just another theory, it's the enlightened perspective, and anyone who awakens from the dreamstate will call it home.

C-Rex is a no-belief-required proposition. You can believe it, I suppose, and you can certainly disbelieve it, but the thing that sets it apart from any and every other theory or model is that it is directly knowable and self-verifiable without the need for any doctrine or dogma, intermediary or intercessor. You don't have to believe it, you just have to stop working so hard not to. This is beyond popular ideas about spiritual development. The old maps and vehicles won't get you here, so it's time to be done with the old and forge the new. The only path is the one you hack out for yourself.

✧

No amount of experimentation can ever prove me right;
a single experiment can prove me wrong. -*Einstein*

C-Rex cannot be objectively proven. Nothing can. The opposite, however, can be done; untruth can be proven. It's called falsifiability. We may not be able to show something is true, but we can show it isn't. The mark of a good model is that it can be easily falsified, and nothing could be more easily falsified than C-Rex.

I observe that when I open the refrigerator door, a light comes on. I have observed this causal relationship one trillion times, and it has done exactly the same thing every time. Based on this I create a hypothesis: When I open the refrigerator door, then the light will come on. That's a valid theory, and like any valid theory, it can never be proven true, but it could possibly be proven false. It can't be proven true because I can never know what will happen in the future, but it can be proven false if, just once, the light doesn't come on. Even if the light *might* not come on, then the theory is defunct, disproven and destroyed. Because the bulb could burn out, or the fridge could lose power, or the sun could go supernova, or a million other possibilities, the light *could* fail to come on when I opened the door, and thus the theory is disproven. The one trillion times it did come on, and the fact that it has never failed to come on, don't prove anything. That's falsifiability. C-Rex is a model, a theory, and must be subjected to the same critical scrutiny.

So, *is* C-Rex falsifiable?

Yes, C-Rex is extremely falsifiable. It's so delicate that the tiniest speck of dust could smash it to bits. We just have to prove that the speck of dust exists and C-Rex is destroyed. All we have to do is prove anything exists and we're done here, but it can't be done. There is no objective reality, there is no proof of a physical universe, and nothing can be proven. The C-Rex model is supremely falsifiable, but it cannot be falsified.

✧

In his stories, Baron Münchhausen claimed to have once lifted himself and his horse out of a swamp by his own hair. This is similar to the Bootstrap Paradox which describes any instance where the foundation for a thing is provided by the thing itself. For instance, consensus reality supports our belief that everyone exists because everyone believes it. This and similar logical paradoxes are sometimes called strange loops and tangled hierarchies. Think of M.C. Escher's drawing of two hands drawing each other, or a corporation owning shares in the corporation that owns it, or the chicken-or-the-egg question, or the phrase used as a chapter title in *Spiritual Warfare*: This sentence is false.

This sort of Möbius strip paradox also occurs when a time travel loop is formed with no discernible beginning or end, like in the *Star Trek* movie where Scottie goes back in time and passes along the formula for manufacturing transparent aluminum, which would eventually be passed down to him so he could go back and pass it along, meaning that transparent aluminum exists without ever having been invented.

Forget it, Jake. It's Chinatown.

Consciousness Defined

> Existence or consciousness is the only reality.
> Consciousness is the screen on which all the
> pictures come and go. The screen is real, the
> pictures are mere shadows on it.

Ramana Maharshi

WHAT IS CONSCIOUSNESS? Ask a hundred recognized experts and you'll get a hundred different answers. I may not be a recognized expert, but my answer is the only correct one. Consciousness is the union of perceiver-perception-perceived. The three are one, no one part stands alone. Without a perceiver, there can be no perception and nothing can be perceived. Without perception, nothing is perceived, so there is no perceiver. Without the perceived, there is no perception and no perceiver. All three must exist together to exist at all. They are one, not three, and the one thing they are is consciousness.

❖

Now it gets tricky. There are actually two types of consciousness; Atmanic and Brahmanic. AC/BC. Atmanic Consciousness is the I Am of the perceiver-perception-perceived dreamstate. Atmanic Consciousness is grounded in Brahmanic Consciousness, which is undifferentiated and absolute; no perceiver, no perception, no perceived. How does untrue Atmanic arise from true Brahmanic? I don't know. Go ask Maya.

Actually, I do know. Untrue Atmanic doesn't arise from true Brahmanic, because untruth does not exist. There is only truth. Brahmanic Consciousness is our absolute nature, Atmanic Consciousness is our living reality. Consciousness is true, the contents of consciousness are not.

❖

Brahmanic Consciousness is without features or attributes. It has no conscience. It is not innately good or evil. It's not moral or spiritual. It has no heart, no bias, no preference, no skin in the game. It's not like the God or gods of our hopes and dreams; it doesn't take sides, it doesn't prefer that you be good or evolve, it doesn't feed on praise or adoration, it doesn't judge or care. Love isn't better than hate, goodness isn't better than evil, pleasure isn't better than pain. Any this/not-that statement we make about consciousness must be false; here/not-there, warm/not-cool, kind/not-cruel, x/not-y, and so on. As soon as we start defining it, we start reducing it to something finite and false.

Brahmanic Consciousness is not just true, it's truth.

❖

Socrates said that the only thing that he knows is that he

knows nothing, but the correct statement is, "The only thing I know is that I exist. I Am." And what is the nature of I Am? Consciousness. I Am and consciousness are synonymous. To say either is to say the other. I-Am/Consciousness is the term we'll use in this document to refer to this single certainty. I exist. I am conscious. I-Am/Consciousness.

I Am is the alpha and omega of knowledge. Nothing else is known or knowable by any conscious entity, anywhere, ever. I Am is the absolute universal constant of knowledge, and there is no other absolute universal constant of anything.

We use the term I-Am/Consciousness in a sort of spiritual legalese. I Am is all any conscious entity could possibly know, but what is the nature of I Am? Consciousness. I-Am/Consciousness isn't two things, it's one thing correctly stated. I Am is the who, and Consciousness is the what; you can't have one without the other, so we christen the new and accurate term I-Am/Consciousness. It can feel a bit bulky at times, like when we start speculating as to your I-Am/Consciousness or other I-Am/Consciousnesses, but I think it's best not to abbreviate this one.

What more can we say about consciousness? Nothing. This is an important point. There are no consciousness experts, and there is no conscious entity in existence or imagination that can know more than I Am. No god or alien or inhabitant of higher planes could know more. Any possessor of I-Am/Consciousness is the equal of any other. There is no greater authority on consciousness than a conscious being, and no one knows more about yours than you. You don't have to earn consciousness, you don't have to go to school or church for it. You are it, it is you. If you understand that consciousness *is* what consciousness is conscious *of*, then you know all there is to know. Any further progress is entirely a matter of decluttering your consciousness by neutralizing emotionally empowered wrong-knowing – ego.

I-Am/Consciousness is the totality of certain knowledge. Everything else is belief and no belief is true. In my few and nap-riddled meditations on the nature of consciousness, I have not come across anything I would consider impossible except knowing more than I Am. This is a rule that can't be broken by any entity of any description on any plane, ever. Adios, Dios.

✧

And speaking of the soul (we weren't, but let's), is there such a thing, or is it just another belief that gets discarded with the rest? And say, hypothetically, that there is such a thing; what would distinguish one from another? Mine from yours?

I-Am/Consciousness is just another way of saying Atmanic/Brahmanic Consciousness. The I-Am part is Atmanic Consciousness, and the Consciousness part is Brahmanic Consciousness. Before the foreslash is self you as you know yourself, and after the foreslash is the truth of you, no-self, which is timeless and undifferentiated and all that. So the good news is, yes, you are immortal in consciousness, but no, the you you think of as you, is not. This might come as unwelcome news for those looking for something a little more personal in the soul department, but on the bright side, Brahmanic Consciousness is an actual thing that actually exists and that you have an actual claim to. Brahmanic Consciousness may be no-self, but it is the truth of you.

This may sound like a cruddy deal to anyone who has a strong sense of selfhood, but after you've whittled selfhood down a bit and seen what it's really made of, you'll be relieved to find anything true under all those layers of false. It's like the tiny dustmote at the center of a fist-sized ball of hail, the seminal something to which the moisture started to cling in the first place. The ball of hail might have an oversized sense of itself until it starts a rapid meltdown to nothingness, but then that tiny bit of dust saves it from oblivion. It may not be a unique ice-rock anymore, but at least it has a claim to existence. It's not nothing.

✧

The God of the Bible, when asked who he was, answered "I Am that I Am". That would be a pretty good answer from you or me, but it identifies this respondent as not-God. A true God must be synonymous with truth and the infinite – Brahmanic Consciousness – which doesn't speak or participate or identify itself as a finite inhabitant of the dreamstate.

✧

As important as knowing what *can* be known is knowing what *can't*. Knowing that no one can know anything is the gateway to knowing everything. The casual observer might assume that we know all sorts of stuff and that science is out there expanding human knowledge every day, but the serious observer finds the library of human knowledge quiet and empty.

Obviously we know what time is, but obviousness aside, the fact is that we have no idea. No one does or can. We go along with our common understanding of time, and time, for the most part, seems fairly well-behaved, but the fact is that no one has any idea what time *is* and no one ever will.

Space? Same thing. It seems too obvious to even question, but it's completely outside anyone's understanding. Energy, matter, bananas, sound, water, whimsy, ethnicity, light, life, two hands clapping, anything you care to name, anything you think you know, will shimmer like a mirage and disappear as soon as you really look at it, because everything that exists within consciousness *is* a mirage.

It is a certainty that any theory, model, philosophy, religion, science or worldview that states or assumes as true anything more than I-Am/Consciousness must be instantly disqualified as baseless speculation. It is a further certainty that any theory, model, philosophy, religion, science or worldview that does *not* state, believe or assume as true more than I-Am/Consciousness must be exactly identical in all respects to the C-Rex model. It's the simple mathematics of truth; when you have beliefs, you are U-Rex dreaming, when you remove all beliefs, you are C-Rex awake.

✧

Consciousness is true, but what consciousness is conscious *of* is not, just as a screen might be solid and the projected images not. The content of consciousness dancing on the screen of mind might be as real and undeniable as a stubbed toe, but not true. This is the immutable truth. It's not theory, guesswork or belief. If you are a conscious entity capable of making the pronouncement I Am, then I-Am/Consciousness is the truth of you and you are capable of knowing this truth directly, and knowing all other knowledge to be baseless and false. It's not spiritual or religious or scientific or philosophical, it just is. Consciousness is, and there is only consciousness.

To the degree that I exist in consciousness, all that I perceive exists in consciousness, so what I am is the same as what everything else is. It's all consciousness. Some of my perceptions may end where my ass meets my chair, but ass and chair and room and sounds and smells and thoughts all reside within consciousness, and to say, as makes sense in U-Rex, that I end here and not-I begins there, is, in C-Rex, baseless and absurd. It's not that me and the chair are the same, but that no distinction between the two arises in the first place. No element of a dream is any more or less real than any other, the only valid distinction to be drawn is between dreamer and dream.

I've observed that some people get hung up on this point. From U-Rex it's hard to believe that a supposedly enlightened person actually experiences unity consciousness, that he sees himself in all things and all that mystical union stuff. Yes, I agree, it sounds bogus, but that's because it's not accurate. It's not that right-knowing moves in, but that wrong-knowing moves out. No good new knowledge rushes in to fill the void left when bad old knowledge rushes out. It's not that I think I'm the same as all I perceive, it would simply never occur to me to think otherwise. I don't perceive artificial distinctions, and there are no real distinctions. Of course it's all one, it's all consciousness.

Mysterium Non Tremendum

> Please be so good as to believe that there is nothing whatever mysterious about this matter. If it were easy, should we not all be Buddhas? No doubt, but the apparent difficulty is due to our conditioning. The apparent mystery, on the other hand, is just an inability to perceive the obvious owing to a conditioned reflex which causes us persistently to look in the wrong direction.
>
> *Wei Wu Wei*

S O WHAT'S THE BIG MYSTERY? From my perspective, everything is visible, everything can be understood, and everything makes sense. Nothing is hidden or withheld. Anyone who *wants* to know *can* know. We are programmed from birth to believe that our existence is an unsolvable riddle, but if we make an effort, then we find that mystery itself is the riddle. Not just *what* is the big mystery, but *why* is there a big mystery? Why is there any mystery at all, and what if there isn't? What if the *mysterium tremendum* is just an internal belief without any external counterpart?

And that's exactly the case. There is no mystery except the one you insist on. It's all you. There is no agent or agency of ignorance keeping you apart from all the great answers of being, they're all sitting out in plain sight with not the least attempt at concealment or conspiracy.

My life has been, in effect, dedicated to the discovery and destruction of mysteries, and I have been completely successful in this. It's not a matter of solving mysteries, but of discovering that they're all just beliefs with no inherent mysteriousness. It's like the gateless gate thing again; once you get past the gate, you see that it was never really there. But as with the gateless gate, getting through in theory and getting through by going through are as different as a desktop globe and planet Earth.

Can C-Rex be grasped theoretically, without making the journey? Sure, maybe, why not. That's what theories are, little postcards we can pass around and admire without the need to actually go anywhere. I understand all sorts of stuff in theory that I really don't understand at all. I understand how GPS works enough to sketch it on a cocktail napkin, but no one flies me in for a consult when one of their navsats goes wonky.

As soon as you start looking at the whole mystery thing, it starts looking wrong. I didn't like all this mystery business long before I ever did anything about it, and when I *did* do something about it, I found that I was right, that all mystery is in the eye of the beholder and that we are free to stop seeing mystery whenever we decide to open our eyes and actually look. This is no small point. We have to look hard at this mystery business in order to get past it. We uncritically accept U-Rex as reality, so we conduct our search for the sun in a cave. Maybe that's the best we can do in U-Rex, but

U-Rex itself is not the best we can do.

✧

We're sitting outside enjoying the crisp morning air. Karl's reading his paper and I'm writing on a legal pad. The twins have been reading some of my rough draft and look a bit confused.

"It's just that reality seems so *real*," John audibly whispers to Claire.

"Yeah," whispers Claire in reply.

They peek up at me to see if I heard and have a response.

"Compared to what?" I ask.

"What?" asks Claire.

"Reality seems so real compared to what?"

They perform a synchronized grimace and turn back to the pages they're reading. A moment later, John has another question.

"Then where does all this come from?"

"All what?" I ask.

"The whole universe," says Claire. "Galaxies and billions of people, China, the Amazon rainforest, cats, dogs, stars, us, I don't know, *everything*."

"And small stuff too," says John. "The whole subatomic world, quarks and leptons, the Higgs thing they're talking about."

"Yeah," says Claire, "and not just now, but stretching out in time, past and future, forever. You can't just say none of it is real."

Karl peers over his newspaper to track the dialogue.

"I agree that it's all very convincing," I say, "but how much are you really conscious of? Are you really conscious of the infinite universe, or just your own small part? I myself am

55

pretty much conscious of what I see and experience and think and dream in the normal course of things. My actual perceptions are really pretty mundane. What I perceive now is typical; some people, some sounds, a small area. And even that overstates it, because all I really perceive is whatever little part I focus on. All this other stuff you mention, galaxies and atoms and whatnot, I only know through pictures or video, or maybe by looking through special lenses, but no one's unaided awareness includes more than we're experiencing right now. So, just as a reality check, check your reality and see if it's really all intergalactic and subatomic, or if maybe it's pretty limited to what you're focused on right now and some blurry peripheral awareness. We might assume we perceive space at the micro and macro levels, and time stretching out infinitely in both directions, but our actual perceptions are a bit less grand."

They seem conflicted, but don't pursue it. After some more time hunched over papers and tablets, both heads pop back up.

"And what is enlightenment again?" Claire asks.

"Freedom from falsehood," I say, "the process of unknowing what is untrue, leaving only the truth in its place. One dismantles one's fictional persona by peeling away the built-up layers of false identity until all that's left is that which can't be severed, destroyed or further reduced; truth, I-Am/Consciousness. Just as truth is ultimately simple, so is I-Am/Consciousness. Easy to understand and no loose ends."

"I think a lot of people would disagree with you," says John.

"About?"

"Consciousness," says Claire, "this whole C-Rex thing."

"Oh, well, absolutely," I say, "I agree with you that a lot

of people would disagree with me, but if you stop and think about it, you'll see that there's really nothing to disagree with. In fact, I'm not really saying anything. I make no assertions or claims, I have no teaching or doctrine. There's nothing to dispute and no facts to dispute with. We're past ideology and beliefs and schools of thought here, past any need for cleverness or scholarship or debate. You're right that a lot of people would disagree that consciousness contains time and space, but they only have belief on their side. Take away belief, and C-Rex is what remains."

"I think you make it sound a little too easy," says Karl from behind his newspaper.

"It's a puzzle with only one piece," I say, "how hard can it be?"

⁜

Once we understand, at least in theory, that all knowledge is belief and that no belief is true, then ridding ourselves of beliefs becomes a straightforward matter of illuminating them and taking away their shadowy power. This is essentially the awakening process. Go through this process to the end, a strange and lonely place called Done, and you will return to a new universe that works in new ways, which makes sense and can be understood, which is responsive and can be interacted with, and which cannot, in any meaningful way, be distinguished from self.

This place where the newly liberated self finds itself is the same universe it was, and the only thing that has changed is that the misunderstanding – wrong-knowing – on the part of I Am has been corrected, and it is now understood that consciousness itself is the grand superset and everything else is just appearance within it. This understanding does not happen with the flick of a switch, but occurs naturally over time as we recompile all the data of a lifetime through a new processor, until the day comes when nuclear war and butterflies and suicide and music and religion and dogs and memories and that scratch on the back of the pew in front of you, are all really, obviously, no belief required, the same.

Unchallenged assumptions are the key to understanding how timeless mysteries are kept mysterious when competent intellects go in search of them. When we begin looking for something beyond the point where it is to be found, then it is forever behind us and our failure to find it is certain. Whether it's the individual searching for meaning, or science searching for a theory of everything, or philosophy searching for truth, the reason that finding answers is difficult is not because they're so well hidden or intrinsically mysterious, but because we begin with false assumptions and head out in the wrong direction to search for things that were never hidden or mysterious at all.

In consciousness, reality is what you perceive. Maybe your reality aligns with consensus and maybe it doesn't; either way, it's your reality. Whatever is, is right. Wrongness is not possible. Even the perception of wrongness is right. Perception is perception, how could it be right or wrong?

Ultimately, we're all afloat on a shoreless sea and no place is any better or worse than another. We want to paddle, though, to move, and Maya has been kind enough to surround us in the illusion of otherness so we can feel discontent with where we are and desire to be somewhere else. We can never understand Maya, but we must be grateful to her. Where would we be without her?

The Story of Markandeya

A LONG TIME AGO, all living creatures had perished. The world was no more than a sea – a gray, misty, icy swamp. One old man remained, all alone, spared from the devastation. His name was Markandeya.

He walked and walked in the stale water, exhausted, finding no shelter anywhere, no trace of life. He was in despair, his throat taut with inexpressible sorrow. Suddenly, not knowing why, he turned and saw behind him a tree rising out of the marsh, a fig tree, and at the foot of the tree a very beautiful, smiling child. Markandeya stopped, breathless, reeling, unable to understand why the child was there.

And the child said to him: "I see you need to rest. Come into my body."

The old man suddenly experienced utter disdain for long life. The child opened his mouth, a great wind rose up, an irresistible gust swept Markandeya towards the mouth. Despite himself he went in, just as he was, and dropped down into the child's belly. There, looking round, he saw a stream, trees, herds of cattle. He saw women carrying water, a city, streets, crowds, rivers.

Yes, in the belly of the child he saw the entire earth, calm, beautiful, he saw the ocean, he saw the limitless sky. He walked for a long while, for more than a hundred years, without reaching the end of the body. Then the wind rose up again, he felt himself drawn upward; he came out through the same mouth and found the child under the fig tree.

The child looked at him with a smile and said, "I hope you have had a good rest."

Jean-Claude Carrière, The Mahabharata

The No-Paradox Paradox

God made everything out of nothing.
But the nothingness shows through.

Paul Valéry

How wonderful that we have met with
a paradox. Now we have some hope of
making progress.

Niels Bohr

I T'S AFTER DINNER ON another beautiful evening. We're sitting in the outdoor livingroom around the dancing flames of the dancing-flames thingy. John and Claire are hunched in conference, Karl is reading a magazine, Sandy is knitting and I have a stack of books I'm trying to plow through. Karl sets down his magazine and looks up.

"What about time travel?" he asks.

"Nope," Claire answers him, "you can't do that."

"Because of the paradox," adds John.

"Because you could kill your parents before they meet," says Claire.

"So your parents couldn't give birth to you," adds John.

"So there would have been no *you* to go back and kill them," says Claire.

"Anything you do could totally change everything," adds John.

"And so on," says Claire.

"Yeah," adds John, "and so on."

"Well?" says Karl to me.

"Well what?"

"What's the answer?"

"What's the question?"

"Time travel. Is time travel possible?" asks Claire.

"Sure," I say.

"What about the paradox?" asks John.

"There is no paradox."

"Paradox!" cries Claire with a grand *j'accuse!* gesture.

"Because if we go back in time..." John says.

"And prevent our parents from hooking up..." Claire repeats.

"Or murder our grandparents..." says John.

Sandy looks up and scowls.

"Okay," I say, trying to nip it before it gets ghoulish. "The paradox you perceive is founded on a false assumption. Revisit what you think you know."

"Like what?" asks Claire.

"What assumption should we revisit?" asks John.

"Time and the arrow of time, for starters," I answer.

"So time travel *is* possible?" asks Claire.

"I'm not sure *im*possible is possible," I say.

"Paradox!" shouts John.

"How about inception?" asks Claire.

"Entering someone else's dream," clarifies John.

"Like the movie," says Claire.

"Going into someone else's dreams and changing what they think," adds John.

"Maybe that's what's happening here," says Claire, "*inception*."

"Maybe you're in our heads messing with our thoughts," adds John.

"Or, maybe you're in your own head messing with your own thoughts," I say.

Claire looks at John to see if that's what he's doing.

"But is it possible?" asks Karl. "This inception and time-travel business?"

"What's not possible in a dream?" I reply. "It would just be your consciousness perceiving and interpreting events like it is right now. Last night I had a flying dream, and it was so real I had a hard time remembering I couldn't fly when I woke up. Samuel L. Jackson screwed me out of five bucks at his pretzel cart, and even after I woke up I had a hard time letting it go. The point is, what does it matter what the content of consciousness is? Flying, inception, time travel, space travel, alien abduction, experience being an insect or a galaxy, experience Godmind or Buddha-mind, whatever, no limits. You are an infinite universe, so what's not possible for you?"

The twins converse quietly for a few moments.

"Then what's the universe again?" asks Claire.

"The dreamstate. Maya's Palace of Delusion. A magnificent

amusement park. Pick a metaphor or create your own."

"But there is no real, actual, physical universe out there?" asks John.

"Of course not," I say. "Where would they put it?"

"So that's a paradox," says Claire.

"No."

"Is it a paradox that it's not a paradox?" asks John.

"Uh, maybe."

They seem pleased.

"What about Zaphod's Infinite Improbability Drive?" asks John.

"It's not his," Claire corrects him, "he stole it."

"He's the president of the galaxy..." protests John.

"That doesn't give him the right to just steal..."

"The Heart of Gold is the president's..."

"No, it's not, he just took it during the..."

"Stop," I say, "please."

They stop. Karl watches. Sandy knits.

"Okay," I say, "if I say yes to the Improbability Drive, will you understand that I'm saying yes to everything?"

"Yes," says John.

"Yes," says Claire.

"Yes," I say.

They break into big grins and look from me to each other and back to me. They seem too pleased, so I scowl at them and they return to their huddle. They are consulting their computer tablets in the hope, I hope, of tripping me up. I return to my book where I'm trying to figure out if Advaita Vedanta or Bishop Berkeley or anyone else has this C-Rex business sufficiently covered already, or if I should really write a book about it.

✧

As long as I'm saying yes to everything, I might as well throw in all the fringe stuff; ESP, UFOs, OBEs, NDEs, trans-this and tele-that, angels and demons, bigfoot, prophecy, astrology, miracles, divination – basically everything from the New Age, Occult and Paranormal aisles. Phenomena that are paranormal in U-Rex, such as perceiving remotely in time and space, are normal in C-Rex. They're simply perceptions, no different from any other. What's not possible in the dreamstate? What can't be dreamt? Perception is the only reality, so if you perceive that something is real, then it's definitively real. There is no other standard by which to judge.

Consciousness is the mechanism by which all things are possible. Take divination, for instance. By what actual mechanism could tea leaves or planetary alignments or chicken gizzards predict the future? In U-Rex, no mechanism could possibly explain such things, so they can't be possible. In C-Rex, the mechanism is consciousness, and such things are just as possible as anything else. Now look at any other paranormal or non-ordinary phenomena, and you'll find that the mystery is unlocked with the same master key. And while we're at it, we might as well take a fresh look at all the normal and ordinary phenomena we thought we understood, because it all works the same way.

✧

Time passes, or so I believe.

"How does consciousness arise from unconsciousness?" asks John.

I look up from a book that I'm glad to look up from.

"Where does that question come from?" I ask.

"We found it online," says Claire. "It's supposed to be one

of the great philosophical mysteries."

"Oh, well, as usual, the assumptions are false, which is probably the better lesson of the question than the answer, which you already know. Consciousness does not exist in time, and since consciousness is all, there's really no alternative to it. There is no such thing as not-consciousness, or other-than-consciousness. That which exists in truth cannot also *not* exist in truth. Would you ask how the infinite arises from the finite? The true from the false? The real from the unreal? *Poof!* Question destroyed, mystery solved. Any others?"

"Why is there something instead of nothing?" asks John.

"That's another great philosophical mystery," adds Claire.

"Good question. Check your assumptions."

"Like what?" asks Claire.

"There are only two," I say.

"That there is something," says Claire.

"And there isn't nothing," says John.

They confer for a moment, then turn back to me.

"This is all pretty confusing," says Claire.

"It's hard to understand," says John.

"There's really nothing to understand," I say. "The difficulty comes from trying to make what I'm saying fit in with what you know, but you can't because what you know isn't right."

That doesn't seem to unconfuse them.

"Without false knowledge," I continue, "C-Rex is easy and natural; no effort required. As I said, this isn't a conceptual challenge for me, it's just where I now reside. If you transitioned from two-dimensional reality to three-dimensional reality, it would be new and confusing at first, but over time you'd get used to it and it would become your new reality. That's how it is for me because I'm here, not because I understand it conceptually. See what I mean?"

They don't look like they do, but don't say they don't.

"Okay, so imagine that you transitioned from two-dimensional reality to three-dimensional reality, and after you got used to it, you went back to describe it to the folks back in two-dimensional reality. One, it would illustrate for you how completely unrelated these two paradigms are, and two, you would have this very challenging and ultimately absurd task of describing your new reality to people, when the only thing worth telling anyone is to come see for themselves. That's where we are now, that's why it's confusing, okay?"

They don't instantly burst into enlightenment. The Zen guys really have a corner on that whole instant bursting thing.

Mountains & Rabbit-Holes

Before enlightenment, a mountain is a mountain.
During enlightenment, a mountain is not a mountain.
After enlightenment, a mountain is a mountain again.

O F COURSE, IT'S NOT A MOUNTAIN, but the universe that is, isn't, and is again. The first line is U-Rex, Maya's palace of illusion. The second line is outside the palace; nothing forever, a strange and lonely place called Done. The third line is C-Rex reality after a decade or so of recompiling and reprocessing.

A mountain is a mountain. = U-Rex Dreamstate
A mountain is not a mountain. = Awake
A mountain is a mountain again. = C-Rex Dreamstate

The third part of this mountain triplet suggests we're back at the first part, but that's not the case. Going into the third phase, the world regains its former reality, but reality itself does not. That second part, where the mountain is not a mountain, is nothing forever. Once all emotionally empowered wrong-knowing is removed, nothing forever is what remains. Nothing forever is *real* reality and this, where you are right now, is *virtual* reality. Transitioning from that second part and settling into the third takes, in my experience, around ten years. Then what? Is the mountain a mountain? Yes, of course it's a mountain, same as it ever was, but no, not really, because no one really returns from nothing forever.

Entering the mountain-again phase, the beholder finds himself in a whole new kind of reality in which, yes, there is a mountain, but, no, there is no mountain. Same mountain, different reality. Perceived and perception haven't changed, perceiver has changed. Wrong-knowing is gone, the filters are removed, emotional connections are severed, the spell is broken.

✦

In *The Matrix*, Morpheus offers to show Neo how deep the rabbit-hole really goes, suggesting that they would be going further down. What he should have said was that he would get Neo out of a hole he was already in. In fact, they never get Neo out, just one level up.

> Before enlightenment, I was in the rabbit-hole.
> During enlightenment, there was no rabbit-hole.
> After enlightenment, I am in the rabbit-hole again.

We don't know the rules in the rabbit-hole because there are none. Is logic logical? Does one plus one equal two? Am

I sane and rational in my belief that I am sane and rational?
I believe my dreams are real when I'm in them, is that
happening now?

I myself have exited the rabbit-hole, and even though I
have re-entered it, I haven't and can't. I am outside even when
I'm inside – sorry about the zenbabble. By exiting the rabbit-
hole, I did not discover who and what and where I really
am, but who and what and where I'm really *not*. There's no
knowledge involved, so it's not the kind of thing that can be
forgotten.

Perhaps the best way to understand mountain-again rabbit-
hole C-Rex is lucid dreaming. Even if we don't experience it,
we can easily understand it; we carry our normal waking
consciousness into the sleeping dreamstate with full awareness
that we are a real person inhabiting an unreal reality.

Mountain is a mountain.	Dreaming
Mountain is not a mountain.	Awake
Mountain is a mountain again.	Lucid Dreaming

The lucid dreamer can snap back into full waking
consciousness in an instant because he never really leaves it.
That's what the lucid part means; we're never fully *in* the
dream like we are in the first stage. We no longer wear a
gown in the madhouse, now we wear a visitor's badge.

The Evil Demon

Am I so dependent on the body and the senses that
without these I cannot exist? But I had the persuasion
that there was absolutely nothing in the world, that there
was no sky and no earth, neither minds nor bodies; was I
not, therefore, at the same time, persuaded that I did not
exist? Far from it; I assuredly existed, since I was persuaded.
But there is I know not what being, who is possessed at
once of the highest power and the deepest cunning, who
is constantly employing all his ingenuity in deceiving me.
Doubtless, then, I exist, since I am deceived; and, let him
deceive me as he may, he can never bring it about that
I am nothing, so long as I shall be conscious that I am
something.

René Descartes

THE EVIL DEMON COMES TO US from Descartes. In coming
up with the cogito, he concluded that an Evil Demon
could deceive him about everything except that he exists. He
has to be correct about the fact that he exists in order to be
deceived by an Evil Demon, so that's the one thing an Evil
Demon couldn't deceive him about.

Descartes' Evil Demon was an expository device, but could there really be such a thing, and is it possible that we live under its sway? An amusing point to make about a mindlink virtual reality like we see in *The Matrix* is that we are probably, as of this writing, within a few decades of being able to feed a digital reality into a living human brain. It's possible that within thirty or forty years, conscious entities could be experiencing full sensory realities without knowing that they're actually just bodiless brains living pre-recorded or computer-simulated lives.

But where would the computer acquire the actual source material from which to render artificial realities? Probably from the decades of digital recording prior to the creation of the mindlink technology, meaning that right now, as I write this, we are living in the narrow band of time from which the data for compiling artificial realities will be harvested. A receiving-mind living inside this mindlink technology would not experience a pre-wired world with no digital recording technology, or a later world in which mind-link technology is familiar and couldn't deceive anyone, but our very own little slice of time. There's only a limited window of time in which to collect the sensory elements of reality, and we're in it.

This means that a reality database could be compiled and would become the core source-material for all mind-link recipients forever; even millennia and further into the future. In terms of a technologically developing society, our timeframe, right now, is the one and only sweetspot for human source-material harvesting. Any receiving mind would find itself living in the first half of the twenty-first century.

And who's to complain about being a receiving-mind? Not you, and as should be clear by now, it's you that we're talking about. That you happen to find yourself living in just this exact period of time, the exact period that will provide the source material for all human artificial reality, is too much of a coincidence to dismiss. What you call planet Earth might have been destroyed eons ago, and your analog life may have been digital all along.

In this light, it's possible that your thoughts and memories are not yours, and that you are not who, what, when or where you think you are. You may not be the species you think you are, and you may have no organic basis at all. You may have never exercised an act of free will, or thought your own thought. Maybe it's not you reading these words and dismissing this idea, maybe it's your original. Maybe there is no you.

The most likely scenario is not like *The Matrix,* where each mind is a separate individual inhabiting a shared computer generated environment. From IT's perspective, that's a terrible and pointless computing nightmare. Much simpler just to call up a file and hit play, so that many minds would be fed a single life. In this scenario, you are one of innumerable minds living the exact same life you're living now, each one certain they are a unique individual, and each one the exact same person – you. This is the most likely scenario. You have no body, just a brain, and instead of a spinal cord and sensory receptors projecting an external world onto your internal screen, you have a cable connecting you to a media player; the digital version of Descartes' Evil Demon.

✥

According to some, it's not just possible, it's probable. Oxford professor of philosophy Nick Bostrom's paper, "Are You Living In A Computer Simulation?" concludes that one of three possibilities must be the case:

1. Humans do not survive long enough to create and run ancestor-simulations.

2. Even if they do, they might choose not to.

3. If not 1 or 2, then any entity with our general set of experiences is almost certainly living in a simulation.

Bostrom states:

If we are living in a simulation, then the cosmos that we are observing is just a tiny piece of the totality of physical existence. The physics in the universe where the computer is situated that is running the simulation may or may not resemble the physics of the world that we observe. While the world we see is in some sense "real", it is not located at the fundamental level of reality.

Who are the overlords of this little scheme, the people one turtle up? Who's minding the minds, and how can they be sure that they themselves are not swimming in an upstream technology? They can't. Bostrom continues:

It may be possible for simulated civilizations to become posthuman. They may then run their own ancestor-simulations on powerful computers they build in their simulated universe. Such computers would be "virtual machines", a familiar concept in computer science. Virtual machines can be stacked: it's possible to simulate a machine simulating another machine, and so on, in arbitrarily many steps of iteration. If we do go on to create our own ancestor-simulations, this would be strong evidence against (1) and (2), and we would therefore have to conclude that we live in a simulation. Moreover, we would have to suspect that the posthumans running our simulation are themselves simulated beings; and their creators, in turn, may also be simulated beings. Reality may thus contain many levels.

Accounting for "arbitrarily many steps of iteration" of

progressively degrading fidelity, no one can ever know if they're an original or a copy, or a copy of a copy, and so on. Nor can anyone know how closely their reality resembles "real" reality. Bostrom takes his Evil Demon scenario further:

> In addition to ancestor-simulations, one may also consider the possibility of more selective simulations that include only a small group of humans or a single individual. The rest of humanity would then be zombies or "shadow-people" – humans simulated only at a level sufficient for the fully simulated people not to notice anything suspicious.

Meaning that you could be here all by yourself.

> There is also the possibility of simulators abridging certain parts of the mental lives of simulated beings and giving them false memories of the sort of experiences that they would typically have had during the omitted interval.

Meaning that you could have been living the last eighteen seconds over and over again for the last eighteen-thousand years, or that you only sprang into existence a moment ago. Once you allow for memory management, anything goes.

All just playful U-Rex speculation, of course. Bostrom himself states that "the implications are not all that radical" and "should have no tendency to make us 'go crazy' or to prevent us from going about our business and making plans and predictions for tomorrow", but anything that helps us disrupt our belief in the reality of reality is a step in the right direction.

Agrippa's Trilemma

> Illusions commend themselves to us because they save us pain and allow us to enjoy pleasure instead. We must therefore accept it without complaint when they sometimes collide with a bit of reality against which they are dashed to pieces.

Sigmund Freud

I AM IS THE ALPHA AND OMEGA OF KNOWLEDGE. Beyond that it's all conjecture without probability. Philosophers may or may not agree with Plato's definition of knowledge as justified true belief, but no belief is true and there is no justification for believing otherwise. Nothing can be known or discovered or figured out beyond I Am. No other knowledge than I-Am/ Consciousness is possible. The God of Wildest Imaginings could not know more.

"But maybe everything we think is true *is* true," says John after reading the previous paragraph to his sister.

"Isn't that a possibility?" asks Claire. "Maybe *everything* is true."

"No, not true," I say, "but you can call it real since it's your reality. In truth all we can say is..."

"I-Am/Consciousness," says John tiredly.

"Yeah," says Claire, "we got that."

"But we must know *more* than that," says John.

"Good," I say, "doubt and skepticism are the appropriate responses. Treat C-Rex as a hypothesis and try to destroy it. Do that with everything anyone tells you; especially me, especially this. I-Am/Consciousness and C-Rex will withstand any attack, but the only way you can know this for yourself is by attacking them yourself."

✧

Behold the egg, it came from a chicken. Behold the chicken, it came from an egg. The question, as we all know, is which came first? And what came before that? And what came before that? And what came before that? And so on. Forever.

In timespace, consensus, U-Rex reality, everything that exists must have a beginning – a time before which it wasn't, and after which it was – and something from which it came; a source or cause, a precursor or progenitor. Anything that exists must have been created, anything that stands must stand *on* something. Any structure must have a foundation to hold it up, but when we look to see what's holding up the structure of our reality, we find three logical impossibilities; Infinite Structure, Self-Supporting Structure, and Magic Structure.

Infinite Structure is bottomless. There is no final, all-supporting support, just endless, unsupportable support. Every new sublevel we insert to support the one above requires another one below. That's infinite regression, and it's turtles all the way down.

Self-Supporting Structure is where the foundation hangs from the structure it supports. You can say, for instance, that you know that God exists because the Bible says so, and the Bible must be right because it's the word of God. That's the circular reasoning fallacy; every chicken came from an egg and every egg came from a chicken. And so on. Forever.

Magic Structure is when we say fuck it, we all see the stupid chicken, it obviously came from somewhere, so let's just say there's a Miracle Egg and leave it at that. That's the axiomatic fallacy, where we insist on a magical foundation – God, the Big Bang, the Great Turtle – and move on. We'll call this the Hissy Defense a bit later on.

And those are the three horns of Agrippa's Trilemma – infinite regression, circular reasoning, the axiomatic fallacy – which falsify the very *possibility* of objective knowledge. The trilemma part is that, unless you can completely ignore the question of being, like my dog does, you have to settle for one of the three, and then employ doublethink to forget the fact that everything you know is based on a lie.

The Difference Between Us

From Spiritually Incorrect Enlightenment.

"…the difference between us isn't something I have that you don't, it's something you believe that I don't. You think it's real and I don't even see it. At this point, I can't even remember it."

"And what's that?"

"Everything. Everything you believe. Everything you're absolutely certain about. Everything you'd bet your life is true."

Curtis knocks on the table. "I'd bet my life this table is true."

"Perfect example," I say. "It would never even occur to me that this table might have reality. I have no thought that even resembles that. I have no context in which such a thought could exist. Reality has no reality for me."

"You're saying there is no table?"

"I'm saying there is no question of a table."

He looks at me speculatively for a minute, trying to figure out if I'm really saying that I don't think the table we're both leaning on is real.

"You're living in the Holodeck," he says, referring to the computer simulated reality environment in *Star Trek*. "Not just the table. Me? The ocean? Everything?"

I let him think about it. He puts it together quickly.

"Computer," he says, "end program."

Moonlight Sonata

Even if you are a minority of one,
the truth is the truth.

Mahatma Gandhi

Truth, like light, blinds. Falsehood,
on the contrary, is a beautiful twilight
that enhances every object.

Albert Camus

A s I TRIED TO MAKE CLEAR IN THE BOOKS, I have no personal interest in expressing this knowledge or in fulfilling the absurd role of spiritual teacher. I do what I do because I exist in a co-creative partnership with some higher thingamajiggy to which I am completely surrendered and entrusted. There is no *me* making decisions, weighing outcomes, pondering imponderables or otherwise setting the course of my life. If I stopped to think about it, I suppose I'd be grateful that it's going this way instead of another way, but even if it went another way, I'd go right along with it.

If you think about it, you'll agree that nothing could make less sense in the lucid dreamstate than doing what I do. If you became fully lucid in your dreams, would you want to spend your time telling dream characters that their reality isn't real? There are only two reasons for doing something so pointedly pointless; either you're programmed/destined/ordained to perform this function, or you're only dreaming that you're lucid; a strangely not uncommon phenomenon.

Ridding oneself of all layers of falsehood leaves one standing naked and alone in an empty place I called Done. Done is the only place where there is no Further. At Done, nothing I was conscious of, myself included, had any substance or reality. Questions were done, knowledge was done, a long period of crackling, hypersane madness was done.

Done is not something that spiritual systems promote or even know about, and it's not what spiritual seekers are seeking. If I was expecting some fantastically awesome pot of gold at the end of the spiritual rainbow, what I found would have had me demanding a refund, but I was never a spiritual seeker, and I knew where everything was going from the First Step, so finding myself in a strange and lonely place called Done was both surprising and expected.

Something else to be said about my own experience is that I had a job. I didn't really begin to understand it until ten years after Done, but I was a smaller part in a larger something, and that larger something, once seen and understood, brought context and meaning to all the smaller parts. The books were that larger something, and once I understood that, the rest made sense. Truth-realization did not make much sense in the story arc of me as a person – or of anyone, since it is impersonal/apersonal/transpersonal – but once the books made themselves known, my life made sense. As much as anything can, anyway.

I consider it my function to express what I understand, and that's what I'm trying to do in this document. It's not my job to frame an airtight legal case or deliver a mathematical proof. My job is to say here it is, the one-and-only perfect theory of everything. Here's how it lays out, here are the hows and whys of it, here's how it's arrived at, and now it's yours if you want it. But you don't get it from a book, or by being smart or committed or spiritual, you get it by stripping away all that is false in yourself.

✢

"You never thought about your new paradigm before the other night when you watched the science show?" Karl asks.

"No, not really."

It's a Friday night and we're sitting outside drinking what Karl calls good beer.

"That seems very strange. For you, I mean."

"Maybe, I don't know. I don't really think anymore. I did kind of a lot of it there for awhile, and since then I have found very little need for it."

"The uncherished sword."

"Uh, yep."

"What about teaching and writing the books?"

"Not the same thing. That was more of an allowing. Maybe there's a difference between creative and destructive thinking, I don't know. Thinking is such a heavy business that I don't do it recreationally or out of curiosity. It's not part of my daily existence at all."

"You don't think?"

"Not the way I think of thinking, no. I view thinking as, well, primitive, clumsy. It was a useful tool back when it was the only tool I had, but I have much better tools now."

"What about C-Rex? Isn't that something you had to think about?"

"Only recently, and not for myself. And it isn't the fun, destructive thinking, just a conversion process. At the end of my own transition I naturally defaulted into C-Rex and everything made perfect sense, so I never felt any urge to dive in and make a study of it. All we're really talking about is reducing a living reality to mere words, and I had no interest in doing that. It never even occurred to me."

"Until you were watching the Science Channel a few weeks ago?"

"Uh, yeah, Maya and I were lying on a bed settling in for a nap when I realized she was giving me a look like I wasn't paying attention to something, so I replayed the previous few moments and realized the guy on the TV was talking about a theory of everything. That was what she wanted me to take note of, and when I did I understood why, and that sparked this current project."

"Maya – the *dog*?"

"Yes."

"Seriously?"

"Yes."

"Okay," he says dubiously, "and before that, this was all so natural to you that you never questioned it?"

"Certainly, the same way your paradigm is so natural to you that you never question it. For what we know and understand directly, words are superfluous and inadequate. I wouldn't try to translate my understanding of things into words any more than I'd try to express the *Moonlight Sonata* in words. Words can only be ridiculously inadequate compared to the actual experience of the music."

"So, then you got this bug in your head and started writing...?"

"No, just notes and research, the real writing started later. I spent the first few days looking into it."

"Like how?"

"Mostly internet, bookstores and a few libraries, trying to determine if what I'm calling C-Rex was already adequately expressed and available, seeing where science is these days, philosophy, religion, spirituality East and West, old and new. Just a long blur of immersion, getting up to speed, seeing if I could derail the project before it got rolling."

"You didn't find anything like C-Rex already available?"

"Not adequately expressed. Not in a way that resembled my experience of it. I think it has to come from someone who lives it, not someone who just theorizes it. Much of what I found was very clever, but lacked authenticity, and really highlighted the difference between theories about a phantom planet, and the direct testimony of someone who calls that planet home."

"So you decided...?"

"No."

"Oh, yes, like the third book?"

"Like all of them."

"So this has all been a big surprise for you."

"Yes, I really thought I was done with all this writing business. In the years since completing the trilogy I haven't thought of anything else to say on the subject."

"Until now."

"Yes and no. I don't think of this material as being part of the trilogy. It seems separate and apart, but once I got started, it seemed like an obvious thing for me to talk about. Anyway, I'm happy to have a little project, and it's clearly something I'm supposed to be doing. Still, I was happy to be done with all this spirituality stuff for the last five or six years, and I'll be glad again when this is done, too."

"Unless there's more."

"Oh yeah, sure, I would never not do something once I saw that it was, uh, you know, indicated."

"On the one hand," he says, "what you are saying about consciousness sounds quite complex, but on the other hand it seems strange that it needs to be said. I wonder why this is not a more common view of reality, why I haven't heard of it before."

I ponder for a minute before responding.

"Well, from the U-Rex perspective," I say, "U-Rex is obviously *real* reality and C-Rex is obviously ridiculous. Also, C-Rex has no upside. There's nothing in its favor, it doesn't go anywhere. Truth is a booby-prize. It doesn't do any good or make anything better. It doesn't provide meaning, it strips meaning away. It takes all the amusement out of the amusement park; no meaning, no significance to anything, no reason to get out of bed in the morning. C-Rex brings nothing to the table, whereas U-Rex creates the illusion of meaning. We must have the context U-Rex provides. Even though it's false, it's still context."

"So the lie is better than the truth, you are saying."

"Sure. The truth might set you free, but then you find yourself standing in an endless parking lot outside the amusement park wondering why you're out, and how to get back in. Truth has nothing to recommend it except that it's true. U-Rex has everything to recommend it except that it's false."

"But here you are," says Karl, "you act, you participate, you contribute to the world."

"The disconnect there is that you think you're talking to a person like yourself, but you're not. I'm a function, a part in a machine. I exist to perform one simple task, and I do my job. I play my role. I experience myself as a person, but I understand myself as a function. I resonate with my function, but I don't resonate with my personhood at all. Does that make any sense?"

He stares at me for a long moment.

"I'm not sure I should be letting you speak with my children," he says.

"Yeah, maybe not."

Science: Our Blind Torchbearers

A billion stars go spinning through the night,
  blazing high above your head.
But in you is the presence that will be,
  when all the stars are dead.

Rainer Maria Rilke

P ERHAPS THE MOST IMPORTANT THING to understand about science as a field of exploration is that it is rigidly paradigm-locked and effectively self-exiled from truth. C-Rex is entirely off the charts of science because the infinite cannot be represented in a finite system. Science is a structure and requires the support that only a false paradigm can provide.

There is no physical universe – period, full stop. A ridiculous statement, perhaps, so it should be easy to disprove, but it can't be disproven. Objective knowledge itself is impossible, meaning that science can never rise above non-probable conjecture. Hence, all science is obviously and inescapably *pseudo*-science.

We could stop right there, but let's not.

✧

I would have thought that the modern-day torchbearers in man's quest for knowledge were graphic novelists and video game designers, but in their book *The Grand Design*, Stephen Hawking and Leonard Mlodinow state:

> Philosophy is dead. Philosophy has not kept up with modern developments in science, particularly physics. Scientists have become the bearers of the torch of discovery in our quest for knowledge.

I suppose Hawking and Mlodinow would rather say that *religion* is dead, killed by science, but they know that religion is not only not dead, but can still bite, whereas philosophy is effectively toothless. Dumping on philosophy might get you some sour looks at the faculty cocktail party, but dumping on religion could get you set on fire – torch-like, ironically.

Has philosophy ever borne any torch? Centuries ago perhaps, during the, uh, enlightenment maybe, and back in ancient days and in the thoughtful East, but if you walk up to anyone nowadays and ask them to which branch or school of philosophy they subscribe, they probably couldn't even make up an answer.

Religion, on the other hand, is a defining aspect of life in any society. Even self-professed atheists reside within a religious ethos from which their rational minds cannot free them, which may be why so many feel the need to self-profess instead of self-shut up.

Right-knowing begins and ends with I Am. The universal religion of U-Rex is *wrong*-knowing, and no wrong-knowledge is better than any other. Science and religion are the two main denominations of wrong-knowing; peacefully opposed, sometimes engaging in petty Skeptic vs Believer skirmishes, both sects representing a pole while the agnostic majority languishes in equatorial indifference, and a wobbly sort of balance is maintained.

Philosophy should reign over both science and religion, but clocks in as an also-ran because it shies away from extreme skepticism. No amount of skepticism could ever be too extreme. The only way to see what doesn't burn is to set everything on fire. But if you *do* burn it all, then you won't be in U-Rex anymore because everything in U-Rex burns – everything except the truth of you.

✧

Let's spare another moment for Stephen Hawking while we're here. There are valuable insights to be gleaned from just the first sentence of *The Grand Design*:

> We each exist for but a short time, and in that time
> explore but a small part of the whole universe.

That might look like a reasonable statement to most people, but anyone conducting a serious search would view it as an unpardonable offense against honest inquiry. If I had been reading this book back when I was trying to get things figured out for myself, I would have thrown it in the reject pile by the first comma, and the authors with it.

Hawking is our most respected scientific guy, and he claims in this same book that philosophy is dead and that science is running point in mankind's quest for knowledge. If it wasn't true that science is bearing the torch for humanity, it would hardly matter, but it *is* true in the sense that a lot of people believe it. Now here's Hawking himself, and the very first sentence of his book is poxy with baseless belief presented as unequivocal fact. Our most respected scientific guy is so infected by his own beliefs that he doesn't know that's all they are. Half a sentence, that's all it takes to unmask the blind torch-bearer. And, in case you're keeping score, not-so-dead philosophy just walked haughty science out to the woods and came back alone. Consensus-based pop philosophy may roll over and play dead on command, but extreme skepticism – aka, honest inquiry – gives no quarter and takes no prisoners.

My advice, as always: BYOFT.

⁘

Karl comes outside and finds me battling Maya on the lawn.

"What are you up to?" he asks.

"I just resolved the conflict between Einsteinian locality and Quantum entanglement, and now I'm showing this person-of-fur who's her daddy."

"Busy day."

The principle of locality states that the only reason something happens to one thing is because the thing next to it made it happen, like dominoes. Quantum entanglement means that stuff changes other stuff at a distance, like sometimes, the first domino can knock down the last domino with none in-between. So which is right?

No one can be right if their assumptions are wrong. There is no locality or non-locality in consciousness, nothing is near or far in space or time. How is it possible that I was in postwar Berlin last night? It's not, but I was. Not really, but it was real.

Maya breaks free of my hold and turns back to me in a posture of bristling readiness, her intense stare alert to my slightest move. At the same instant, we lunge.

The next round goes to her.

✧

We expect a theory of everything to come from physicists, probably because they're the ones who keep prattling on about it, but they're not really talking about a theory of everything, just a theory of the universe, which is not only not *every*thing, it's not *any*thing.

> Atoms are the fundamental building blocks of everything
> that we can see, so if you understand the atom, you
> understand the universe.   -Michio Kaku

That's like saying that if we can understand the bricks that make up a house, we will understand the family living inside. Right there, in a single sentence, we see how far science falls short. We're mapping genomes and neural networks and distant space because it's less scary than figuring out how my dog knows when I'm staring at her, but how my dog knows when I'm staring at her is *much* closer to a fundamental building block of everything than any atom or God particle could ever be.

Scientists put so much emphasis on reproducible results for experimental validation that they sometimes mistake non-reproducibility for non-validity. Reproducibility may validate, but *ir*reproducibility does not *in*validate. Nor is something disproven, as is frequently insinuated, just because it hasn't been scientifically proven.

My living reality is shaped by a dynamic transpersonal interplay that is no less real because it can't be tested or repeated under controlled conditions. For me, conscious interactivity with reality is far beyond the occasional brush with serendipity; it's my sole mode of earthly navigation. It is constant and unfailing, and as real to me as anything could be. It's how I operate in the world; how I accept and reject, want and allow, see and know. It's how I interface with reality. I know others for whom this is also true and we understand each other perfectly when speaking of how things "really work". However, as normal as this mode of operation might be to me and others, it is definitely paranormal by normal standards. My experience is evidence – though only to me, of course – that regardless of anything else, consciousness and reality are interwoven, and that anyone who says otherwise, by commission or omission, does not merit further attention. I think most people have enough direct experience of non-ordinary phenomenon to know that any group or ideology that rejects it should be rejected.

When supposedly skeptical atheists and scientists pick on monotheistic religion in books, speeches and debates, they are simply beating up a court jester in a clown crown. They think that by clobbering the clown of religion, they have overthrown the kingdom of transphysical reality, but such arguments cannot sway anyone established in the integrated, co-creative state, which is the serious reality underlying the circus of religion.

❖

I enjoy science as much as the next guy who doesn't care much about science, but here's the thing; science isn't representing our interests. Not mine and probably not yours. It could, but it isn't.

We have mountains of subjective reports of every kind of paranormal and non-ordinary phenomenon you could imagine, and there is more than adequate evidence for much of it. On top of that, there are the explorers of the inner realms, the entheonauts and mystics and shamans and the rest, providing highly credible reports of inner worlds which they often describe as more real than our normal waking reality. On top of that, there's the stuff that anyone can go bust a toe on, like thousands of structures worldwide of such mystery and complexity that they are beyond our abilities to fathom or reproduce today. And then there's the rest of it, all the cool, great, interesting, unexplained stuff that is of the very essence of this human experience. How many pretty pictures of distant galaxies do you really care about? Of what real value to you are Higgs bosons or the eleventh dimension or superstrings? What has the space program ever given you except an amusing but forgettable hour in an IMAX theater?

And then there's death. Isn't it pretty likely that there's something more there than meets the eye? (Hint: If consciousness exists and time doesn't?) Doesn't that seem like a good place to put some serious scientific attention? Not by pushing it further away with pills and scalpels and radiation, and not by further monetizing our fear of it, but by treating the subject with some respect and shining some bright lights on it. This is where people want to see their torchbearers working up a sweat, not dangling from corporate coattails.

By simply acknowledging the obvious fact that there is no

such thing as objective reality, science could tear down its self-erected walls and get in the game. Science, meet crop circles. Play nice. Let us know when you come up with something better than the Merry Planksters. And when you've got that sorted out, we have about eight-hundred other very real questions you might be able to answer. Cut loose the space station, bulldoze the colliders, and let's get to work on the real mysteries; not the ones that exclude consciousness but the ones that begin with it, the ones that might actually help us make sense of things or make life better for people or advance the dialogue.

The real point isn't that science should, could or would stop goofing around and get serious, it's that anyone who wishes to be serious and figure out their own situation must cross science off their list of go-to guys. To whatever degree we might trust science to represent our interests, it's important that we revoke that trust in order to move forward.

✧

One of the amusing things that comes with the C-Rex model is a reversal of respectability. Now all the fun, weird stuff moves from lunatic fringe to front-and-center, while science, philosophy and religion take up their rightful place on the blurry outskirts of human interest. Science goes from serious and respectable, to obsolete and irrelevant, while all the nutty paranormal stuff becomes the main attraction. We have guys like Hawking declaring that science is the torchbearer for humanity, and that might be true at the herd-level, but if you get away from the core herd a bit you start to see where the real work is being done, by the real torchbearers out on the fringe and beyond, including a surprising number of open-minded scientists.

✧

Are scientists our greatest minds? Maybe, but moot. Great intelligence and effective thinking seldom go together. In fact, not only are scientists *not* our best thinkers but, due to years of highly specialized education and training, they are probably the most narrowly focused and effectively indoctrinated people in the modern world. This is as it must be, but such intense focus automatically disqualifies scientists from addressing the broadest questions of being. As Richard Feynman said, a scientist looking at nonscientific problems is just as dumb as the next guy.

✧

All scientific claims should be prefaced with a disclaimer. That seems like a scientific-y thing to do. A standard disclaimer would probably suffice in most cases:

> WARNING:
> The scientific findings contained herein are based on the uncritical acceptance of consensus reality as true reality, and must therefore be viewed in the same light as mythology, folklore, superstition and religion.

But, as honest as it might be to provide this disclosure, science can't afford to acknowledge its operating assumptions. Those assumptions are what holds science up, and no one wants to cut the branch they're sitting on.

I suppose that any scientist would dismiss my assertions as laughable, but they can't do it scientifically. They can't falsify C-Rex and they can't prove anything, making science the most radical of fundamentalist religions. We have to make every effort to understand this directly because science *is* the presumptive torchbearer of human knowledge, and much of the wired world is kneeling in their church.

It's not my wish to deliver an anti-science polemic, but to encourage the reader to take a fresh look at the overhigh esteem in which we hold science. If you think that all this I-Am/Consciousness and C-Rex business is fine for quirky fringe thinking, but that the real load is being carried by the guys who fill chalkboards with arcane formulae or put wires in rat brains, then those are your Buddhas and those are the guys you need to kill. *(Metaphorically! Don't make me... aw hell, whatever.)*

Serious thinking is corrosive to the layers of lies in which we insulate ourselves, including our very selfhood, and most people, even the ultra-smart, would do anything rather than subject themselves to prolonged and repeated acid baths. Honest thought is invariably destructive and must ultimately result in untruth-unrealization and C-Rex. In any case, none of this truth, adulthood, or C-Rex stuff requires super-intelligence, just serious thought and intent.

We're way out in uncharted waters with this C-Rex stuff, and it's every man for himself. It's not my job to convince anyone of anything; this is way past that kind of thinking. I can hold it up, but you have to come get it. You have to approach this with no other agenda than personal understanding of personal reality. Yes, it's difficult to believe that scientists can't even play in their own sandbox, but they can't, and that's a scientific fact.

Religion: The Magic Turtle

An error does not become truth by reason of
multiplied propagation, nor does truth become
error because nobody sees it.

Mahatma Gandhi

I N MY MOUNTAIN-AGAIN RABBIT-HOLE, the thing I find
most unbelievable is belief. If I were in an elevator with
a Christian, Muslim, or Jew, I think I could, like some
spiritual decongestant, remove mental mucous and restore
free thinking in thirty seconds. I know that's not true, but
that's how thin and unconvincing religious belief appears to
me. I can't reconcile it. I can't really believe that anyone really
believes it.

I'm convinced that if we took the most devout believer out of their belief-conducive environment for a month, away from all their trappings and trinkets, their programs and rituals, away from their codependents and enablers, away from triggers and support systems, away from all the little ways we empower fictions that have no power of their own, then that person, along with my thirty-second elevator pitch and a few moments of honest reflection, could return to the world disabused of their religious affliction, and a real step closer to adulthood.

Nonsense, of course, but that's the weird thing about having truth on your side; you start to think it counts for something. It doesn't, but because truth is better than anything anyone could make up, you get this false sense of what it could do if unleashed upon a sleeping world, like you could just pry people's eyes open and they'd have to see. Even as I write this, I know that's not true, but I don't know why.

That's what my primary realization did for me. It pried my eyes open to the simple and obvious fact that the swamp of eternal delusion couldn't be all there was. There had to be something else; a place where something made sense. That place was truth, and the ridiculously simple realization that truth exists made me grab a six-inch knife and jump out of my rickety little boat into a churning ocean of blood and froth in a hopeless bid to slay an enormous and unslayable beast. That's why I'm so wrongly convinced that the same realization could have the same impact on anyone of sound mind and stout heart. You can't find truth in the swamp, but that doesn't mean there is no truth. Before you can be blown apart by the realization that truth exists, though, you have to realize that you don't have it and it's nowhere in sight, and that's the white-hot realization from which belief shields us.

Monotheistic religions can't survive on their own merit so their time-tested strategy is to abandon common sense and be so über-nutso that they can't be held to any reasonable standard of reason. This approach works for them, but it's not of their creation or devising. It's a facet of life in the fogbound, eyes-closed, fear-based dreamstate, and the soil in this part of the amusement park is so fertile that virtually any story you plant will sprout into an inhabitable fantasy. If you live in such a fantasy alone, you're mentally ill, if you live there with a small group, you're a brainwashed cultmember, and if you live there with a large group, you're respectably religious.

I can only speak in general about monotheistic religions because whenever I swoop in for a closer look I get lost in the muck and mire and have to rise back out. Stated less metaphorically, the only thing I understand in U-Rex is that nothing in U-Rex can be understood. There is no clarity possible in this interminable swamp, no possibility of anything more than more and more swamp. That's why scientists and scholars and philosophers can dig and probe and sift forever and never reach an end. You can say the inhabitants of this swamp have their eyes closed, or that they're fogblind, but the result is the same; no one can see anything, including the fact that no one can see anything.

Nothing can ever make sense in this swamp. That's why we're not doing any mudwrestling in this document; there's never any point in engaging beliefs at their own level. Nor do we need to borrow their validity with one hand while invalidating them with the other. For instance, we don't need to cite elements of quantum theory to bolster C-Rex so it can then invalidate quantum theory.

✧

The four broad categories of belief-system are philosophy, science, spirituality and religion. Religion is the strongest because it's primarily emotional. However, it's also the least credible and requires the most external reinforcement. It's easy to see how someone might think light exists, or that Plato was a toga'd rockstar, or that meditation with a Zen motif can constitute a vehicle to somewhere, so those belief systems can chug along on their own steam, but the monotheistic religions are so intellectually flaccid that they can only remain erect by artificial means. The means is emotion and the emotion is fear.

Ultimately, of course, philosophy, science, and spirituality are no better than religion. There is no such thing as light, Plato played air guitar, and no amount of meditation can get you anywhere because there's nowhere to go. Scientists might suppose themselves the sanest or least gullible because they have facts on their side, but their facts are written on the back of a giant turtle right alongside the facts of the immaculate conception and the virgins-for-killers incentive program.

Yes, fine, but what does any of this have to do with a theory of everything?

This: The defining feature of a monotheistic worldview is One Almighty God. It's a short step from saying that there is One Almighty God to saying that One Almighty God is a theory of everything – the prime mover, the uncaused cause, the magic turtle that supports unsupported. No, it doesn't make sense, but it doesn't have to, that's the magic part. Religions don't have to stand on their own merit because they're supported by the emotional buttressing of millions of needy believers.

Which is *not* to say that there's no *there* there. If, as has been said, all religions contain a core truth, then the reality underpinning the religious experience is the same reality underpinning everything; overlighting intelligence, energy, flow and obstruction, co-creation, our direct connection to the absolute and infallible. The degree to which we are able to surrender ourselves and disempower ego is the degree to which we are able to let ourselves be guided, informed and enriched by this overlighting intelligence. In holy books this surrender appears as Thy Will be Done, Brahma is the Charioteer, the Will of Allah. This is the underlying reality of being, and anyone should be able to see this in their own life regardless of how much ego they pile over it. Anyone can see patterns unfold, desires manifest, prayers answered; the trick is to see what's there and no more. What's there is enough; we don't need to use it as a foundation for cockamamie belief systems.

And that's what they don't know in the swamp. They don't know that truth exists – that they don't have to make it up.

Philosophy West

How vain it is to sit down to write when
you have not stood up to live.

HD Thoreau

You can't cross the sea merely by standing
and staring at the water.

Rabindranath Tagore

C-REX IS BLEEDING EDGE PHILOSOPHY, and yet, it's nothing
original theory-wise. The paradigm I call C-Rex might
be known in Western philosophy as Monistic Idealism or
Subjective Immaterialism or somesuch. If we had to give
the C-Rex model a proper philosophical title, it might be
Idealistic Antimaterialistic Monism; IAM. Monism means
there's only one thing, Idealistic means the one thing is
thought, and Antimaterialism means we needed an A to form
the clever acronym (it means the physical universe doesn't
exist). A mouthful like Idealistic Antimaterialistic Monism
should help you appreciate the brevity of C-Rex.

When we look at Western philosophy, we see little more than armchair academics whose guiding light is not truth, but reputation and career. They have nothing to contribute, so they are effectively confined to clucking at each other and denying their irrelevance. A living philosophy is a journey of the most extreme proportions; a personal inferno, prolonged and bitterest conflict. To take just a single step on this journey is to leave the petty concerns of success and self-image behind forever, so yes, philosophers are non-participants and ideologues. They suit up like players and talk a good game, but never take the field.

⁕

I think I think, but do I really think? I think so, but I don't *know* so, and as I open myself up to the possibility that I *don't* think, it starts looking more like a probability, and maybe a certainty. Am I just perceiving that I think? Do my perceptions and interpretations of perceptions have any trustworthy basis? Of course not.

In print, it all looks too confusing, like no one could actually live their life like this, but I do, and it's not confusing at all. What I see and remember about U-Rex is that nothing makes sense and everything is confusing. In C-Rex, it's just the opposite, nothing is confusing and everything makes sense; no vexing riddles or paradoxes or imponderables, no violations of reason or common sense, no belief required. The C-Rex perspective isn't something I have to think about, it's just is-ness uncontaminated by wrongness. There are no conflicts, no points of confusion, no dark, scary corners. Without false beliefs and attachments to preconceptions, everything just opens up to a state of constant flow and revelation.

I don't concern myself for thirty seconds a year with all

this truth and perception business. My paradigm is a non-issue to me, just as yours is to you. Recent events have caused me to sit down and attempt to express my worldview in two-dimensional symbols, so that's what I'm doing, but I barely recognize my living reality in these flat words. It all sounds terribly complicated and unlikely, but then I return to my direct experience of it, and it all becomes simple and obvious again.

✧

Solipsism, the theory that only the self can be known to exist, is sometimes called the third rail of Western philosophy; if you touch it, your reputation and career die. This makes sense because solipsism is a philosophy killer. Philosophers cannot acknowledge the simple and obvious truth of solipsism, because solipsism reveals that philosophy can never rise above non-probable speculation. Even to be distantly connected with solipsism might stigmatize a philosopher's career and reputation forever. This, of course, reflects not on solipsism itself, which is beyond dispute, but on Western philosophy, which is unable to venture into truth just as shadow is unable to venture into light. Philosophy dwells in the halflight of shadows and mystery, and ceases to exist in the full light of truth where everything is plain and simple, and where no mystery remains to be philosophized about.

✧

As John and Claire pointed out, one of the most fundamental of all philosophical questions is, Why something instead of nothing? Why is there creation at all? It's always valid to question the question. How do we know there is something?

And what is this something we know there is? Of course, this just loops you back to consciousness and the inevitability of C-Rex. The unstated assumption in this question is that nothingness, or non-existence, is a primal state, or at least a possible one. Cosmologists support this view by asserting that prior to the big bang was nothingness, in which neither time nor space nor physical laws existed. This pre-bang nothingness resembles Brahmanic Consciousness and the post-bang resembles Atmanic Consciousness. Just kidding, nothing about the big bang makes any sense, of course, it's just a prime-mover expedience like the Hindu who insists that the turtle supports unsupported, or the monotheistic assertion that God is the uncaused cause. We can't build anything without a foundation, so we have to tie off those tiresome regresses, even if we have to employ doublethink to do it.

So, why something instead of nothing? In C-Rex the question self-destructs. You could say that it's not a valid question because there actually *is* nothing and *isn't* something, or, at least, that the assumption that there *is* something and *isn't* nothing is baseless. Or, you could simply say the only thing you can say about consciousness: Consciousness Is. With time as a subset of consciousness instead of the other way around, there is no longer any question of alternatives to Is-ness. There is no before or after, beginning or end, then or now – there is only the infinite *is*.

One better-than-it-sounds answer to the question, Why something instead of nothing?, is simply, Why not? It sounds like an evasion, but since the correctly stated question is, Why Consciousness?, Why not? seems like as good an answer as any, and it never hurts to put the ball back in the inquirer's court and make him do the work. Wouldn't you agree?

Another common question is, why are we conscious at all? This is like asking why water is wet. Wetness is what water is. They're inseparable. Consciousness is what I am; essence, not attribute. To ask *why* I am conscious is to assume a distinction between self and consciousness, to assume the possibility of one without the other, like assuming the possibility of dehydrated water. (The next Pet Rock!)

Just as truth exists and untruth does not, consciousness *is* and other-than-consciousness *is not*. Being conscious is not a facet of some larger, independent me, it's my very me-ness and there is no larger anything. It's not that I am conscious, it's that I am conscious*ness*. I-Am/Consciousness.

✧

In researching for this document, I read (skimmed through) some books by noted scientific and religious thinkers. I also viewed (skipped through) some lectures, symposiums and debates by representatives of the scientific and religious communities. The speakers were respected educators and authors, but their debates seldom proved more insightful than any believer vs non-believer argument you might overhear in a bar. There's just not much to say, and the arguments don't improve with pedigree. Believers believe in belief, scientists believe in science, and the collision of these titans results in little more than a moderated pillowfight. In a surprising number of these dialogues and debates, philosophers were conspicuous by their absence, leaving science and religion to quibble without the unreasonable demands of reason.

Sad-making is the term I use in situations like these, (ensaddenating sounds silly), where so much potential goes so unrealized. It's a particular shame that the belief faction is usually saddled with Christianity and the Bible. It seems like Christianity is all soft underbelly and science is all sharp scalpel, but the belly is enormous and the scalpel is tiny, so both sides get more winded than wounded. It would be much more interesting to see Science vs Logic, where science would be pressed to state its assumptions and be revealed for the baseless belief system it really is, most akin to a fundamentalist cult. We'd never see that bout though, because it wouldn't go past the weigh-in. Ponderous, lumbering Christianity is about all that science and atheism can handle.

My original purpose in following this line of inquiry was to see if anyone was making a case against the case I was making. That's not a serious concern, but I do worry a little because I'm not sure that I'm not insane. Mainly, I guess I was looking for interesting insights, compelling arguments, a worthy ally or foe, unexpected frankness, deviations from the standard patter – but alas, no joy. Science will admit that it operates under certain assumptions, but that's as honest as it gets. That's the ensaddenating part; that the West's highest level of dialogue is perpetually stuck in the basement.

Alas again, it's not for me to say, but for you to see. We think we are fully conscious, we think we are awake, we think we think, but those thoughts are based not on thinking, but on not thinking. We never look because we never doubt, and we never doubt because we accept appearances and ride on the tide of consensus.

I'd advise you to consider reconsidering your views on humanity itself. I know how it looks from the inside, how it seems like we have our brightest people working on the biggest issues; science is sorting out God particles and theories of everything, philosophers are hard at work unraveling the great mysteries, and the magical religions have magical answers. The general view is that we are intelligent and capable, and that we have our best people dedicated to getting these big-ass mysteries solved for us. This is the safe refuge that lifts the burden from us by shifting responsibility to non-self agents and agencies, but to get anywhere we have to take on the full burden, so it's useful to understand that no one is out there getting this stuff figured out for you. You are the only one representing your interests. Do it yourself or it don't get done. BYOFT.

Philosophy East

The only truth is I Am - I Exist. That is the only truth.
Everything else is a concept.

Ramesh Balsekar

The Perennial Philosophy is expressed most succinctly in the
Sanskrit formula, *tat tvam asi*; the Atman, or immanent
eternal Self, is one with Brahman, the Absolute Principle of
all existence; and the last end of every human being, is to
discover the fact for himself, to find out who he really is.

Aldous Huxley

T HE MOST VALUABLE CONCEPTS we can take from the East
are Brahman, Maya and Atman. There are others, but
don't get greedy or you'll end up like that monkey who
couldn't get his hand out of the jar because he wouldn't release
the banana. The real fool's gold is found in the pockets of the
drowned.

Most notable among Eastern philosophies for our purposes is the idea that Brahman Is All, where Brahman is without attributes and therefore precisely synonymous with any term we define as without attributes, such as truth or consciousness. Saying Brahman Is All just means we're using the word Brahman instead of consciousness. Here we're calling it consciousness because I experience consciousness directly, and I don't know this Brahman guy from Adam.

✧

Advaita Vedanta is the philosophical pinnacle of Eastern thought (and, therefore, of world thought), but Advaita is like Buddhism and Zen for me; as soon as I enter, everything that lured me in turns into something else. From the outside it looks okay, but as soon as you go in, you find yourself right back in Maya's house of mirrors. My distinct impression is that many adherents and promoters of Advaita and nonduality completely misunderstand both what it is and what it's not.

Brahman is Atman, Atman is Brahman. That's the whole deal. Truth has no teaching, requires no guru, and is not a spiritual pursuit. That bears repeating: Truth is not a spiritual pursuit. A guru may be necessary to follow a teaching, but to make a journey we must cut everything away, gurus and teachings included. We can sit together, but we must travel alone. If you think you see more in Advaita, or any teaching, then look down and watch those vines wrapping around your ankles.

Remember, there's nothing to know. Kill the guru. No head full of spiritual knowledge or wall full of spiritual books can ever be other than an anchor. All forward motion depends on release, not gain. Only that knowledge which destroys knowledge facilitates progress. Don't seek external validation, be your own guru. Students don't make journeys and travelers don't sit in classrooms. This little caution bears emphasizing because our compelling tendency toward spiritual inertia is why the most spiritually knowledgeable, respected, and dedicated, are not themselves awake.

If you want to understand Maya, if you want to make sense of the dreamstate, if you want to reconcile the irreconcilable, then you are consigning yourself to a lifetime of blind wandering, like countless billions before you. You can believe something new every week, or one thing for the rest of your life, but you will never discover the slightest trace of true knowledge. You'll be in good company, though, if that counts for anything.

✢

To digress a bit, I feel at times like I'm delivering a message more appropriate to the trilogy than to this theory-of-everything document. That's probably because I don't buy into the whole theory thing. Concept-level understanding seems to me like a dream within a dream, but I don't know why anyone would want to do anything but wake up.

Well yes, I do know, but, as always, I feel that I'm not communicating so much with the reader as with the reader's little bastard, that muffled shrieker and spiritual anarchist who wants to stage a coup and throw firebombs and blow the dreamstate all to hell. That little bastard is alive in you, and he wants you dead. I see him as the good guy in all this, the scrappy underdog, and maybe someday he'll make you grab that six-inch knife and jump out of the boat and begin the journey beyond self.

However, to continue this digression a bit more, I will repeat what I said in the books, which is that Human Adulthood is the real prize for everyone everywhere. That's what all spiritual seekers really want, not truth or enlightenment, and that's what absolutely everyone should pursue at all costs. No shit.

✧

Here, we take a description of Brahman, and replace the word Brahman with Consciousness:

> Consciousness is the One, the whole and the only reality. Other than Consciousness, everything else, including the universe, material objects and individuals, are false.

> Consciousness is at best described as that infinite, omnipresent, omnipotent, incorporeal, impersonal, transcendent reality that is the divine ground of all Being.

> Consciousness is often described as "not this, not this" because Consciousness cannot be correctly described as this or that. In fact, Consciousness can never be known as an object of experience because it is the very subject that experiences everything.

> Consciousness is the origin of this and that, the origin of forces, substances, all of existence, the undefined, the basis of all, unborn, the essential truth, unchanging, eternal, the absolute.

> How can Consciousness be properly described as something in the material world when Consciousness itself is the basis of reality?

> Consciousness is the substrate of the material world, which in turn is its illusory transformation. Consciousness is not the effect of the world, but its very cause. Consciousness is said to be the purest knowledge itself, and is illuminant like a source of infinite light.

Due to ignorance, Consciousness is visible as the material world and its objects.

Consciousness is attributeless and formless. It is the Self-existent, the Absolute and the Imperishable.

✧

Another significant concept we can borrow from the East is Maya; that which allows us to see what's not and not see what is. Without Maya, there is no U-Rex, no amusement park, no you and me. Here again we replace the word Brahman with Consciousness:

Maya is the complex illusionary power of Consciousness which causes Consciousness to be seen as the material world of separate forms.

Maya has two main functions; one is to "hide" Consciousness from ordinary human perception, and the other is to present the material world in its place.

Maya is also said to be indescribable, though it may be said that all sense data entering one's awareness via the five senses are Maya, since the fundamental reality underlying sensory perception is completely hidden.

It is also said that Maya is neither completely real nor completely unreal, hence indescribable. Maya dwells within Consciousness, but Consciousness is unaffected by Maya, just as a magician is not tricked by his own magic.

Maya is temporary and is transcended with "true knowledge," or perception of the more fundamental reality, Consciousness, which permeates Maya.

✧

Decades ago, back when I still formed pointless opinions

about irrelevant stuff, it seemed obvious to me that everything interesting about India arose from Soma, probably *psilocybe cubensis*, and that nowadays, without their sacred-potion precursor, India is just the ghost town of an extinct people who were once the coolest hippies of all time. Soma makes Hinduism make sense, and the Vedas rave about Soma, so it seems like we can make that connection. Furthermore, when we look at modern day Hinduism, we see that it is lacking the living sacrament that connects its adherents directly, rather than just providing a bunch of second- and third-hand "knowledge" devoid of living context. So, just another dead religion, but at least this one has some actual basis in the annals of courageous consciousness.

✧

Besides Advaita, the lifetime work of mystic mathematician Franklin Merrell-Wolff should be mentioned here, if only to likewise spare the reader from spiritual tire-spinning. What we're calling Brahmanic Consciousness, Merrell-Wolff called consciousness-without-an-object, or the Great Space. Of Merrell-Wolff's 56 *Aphorisms on Consciousness-Without-an-Object*, we can take 1 and 56, and leave 2 through 55.

   1. Consciousness-without-an-object is.
   56. Beside the Great Space there is none other.

Truth exists, untruth does not. There is only truth.

Philosophical Zombies

Mommy always told me,
  Son, don't never trust a zombie.
Oh, but Mommy, you're a zombie too,
  Who can I trust if I can't trust you?
Mommy is a zombie, whatever shall I do?

I KNOW I-AM/CONSCIOUSNESS, but I don't know You-Are/Consciousness. I don't know anything about you except that I perceive you. In this sense, you are just another element in my conscious environment, as real or not-real as a thought or a memory or a dream. I might treat you like I believe you possess I-Am/Consciousness, but I have no idea. Here in the rabbit-hole, I'm just going along to get along. I have learned that if I don't kick big rocks, I don't suffer the ill-effects thereof. When in Rome, and all that. Assuming for the moment that you *do* possess I-Am/Consciousness, then I am to you as you are to me; a perception, the appearance of a person, a Philosophical Zombie.

Only you know if you exist, but you have no idea about anyone else. In philosophy, this is called the Problem of Other Minds, and the Philosophical Zombie thing is a real tool for understanding that perceived entities – everyone else – cannot be assumed to possess I-Am/Consciousness. They could just be non-sentient actors playing their roles on the stage of my dreamstate – my dreamstage. For all our feelings of community and connectedness, the existence of other people can never be more than a non-probable belief.

I say again – it would be hard to overstate this point – that no mystic or deity or high-placed insider could ever know more than I Am. However you reckon the universe, whatever you believe, no one can ever know more than you know. There is no greater authority in the universe than you. If you know I Am, then you have reached the Knowledge Maximum. Well done, I'm sure your parents would be very proud, if they actually existed.

For me, the main argument in favor of other people, other I-Am/Consciousnesses, is that infinite intelligence, which I allow myself to wink at, strongly suggests it. So, if I'm pretending that infinite intelligence is true, and since I'm speculating the apparent world anyway, and since it doesn't really matter, I might as well pretend that other conscious entities exist. Outside the rabbit-hole, away from Maya, there is absolutely no you or me or anyone else, but in the rabbit-hole, life is a whole lot more comfortable if you relax and play along.

Okay then, what about higher or more evolved beings? Inhabitants of subtler planes? Higher vibration, less physical beings? The channeled guys and the higher selves and the oversouls and whatever else? Do they exist? In truth, the answer is no. In the rabbit-hole, the answer is unknowable.

We can grant the possibility that other entities exist, but what we can't grant is the impossible, and impossible would be any entity knowing more than I Am. Therefore, any other beings, no matter how subtle or advanced, would necessarily be like us; inhabitants of a false paradigm, defined by false beliefs. What does that say about these higher entities that we speculate might exist? It says that they are just inhabitants of the broader amusement park, and if they do exist, they must be of the same essential nature as we are. They might even inhabit a different paradigm, but that different paradigm is either C-Rex, or it's false. Ultimately, false-knowledge is all that could possibly distinguish any one conscious entity from any other. Because all I can ever know is I Am, I can never be certain that I am not the only conscious entity in existence – the sole beholder.

Could there be something other than false-knowledge that distinguishes two hypothetical beings from each other? Maybe, but now we've wandered off into the infinite gray sprawl of speculation where every step changes everything, and where no certainty, or even probability, can ever be found. That's what happens when we start trying to reconcile the irreconcilable and beat some sense into what-if scenarios; we get lost before we know we strayed. It might seem like we're talking about completely obvious things that everyone agrees on, but since the existence of other people never rises above the level of baseless speculation, their agreement fails to tip the scales.

The real point is not to make better sense of appearances, but to understand that appearances are nothing more than nothing. No perception is more true than any other. Everything in the apparent universe possesses an exact and knowable value: I Am is one, everything else is zero.

The Great Objection

This is patently absurd; but whoever wishes to become a philosopher must learn not to be frightened by absurdities.

Bertrand Russell

When truth is evident, it is impossible for parties and factions to rise. There never has been a dispute as to whether there is daylight at noon.

Voltaire

T HE MAIN OBJECTION TO C-REX is that it's ridiculous. It's complete and utter nonsense. Only a fool could believe such twaddle, baloney, rubbish, hokum, poppycock, hooey — you get the idea. Fair enough, it's a bunch of nonsense. So, how do I respond to this objection?

I agree. Completely. As poppycocky as you want to say it is, I'm with you. I make no objection to this objection. This theory of everything, C-Rex, is simply, obviously, bullshit.

Agreed.

But now, before we address this objection, are there any others? Is there anything else to be said against the C-Rex model other than the fact that it's too ridiculous to be taken seriously?

No, there is not, and this is a very important point. The only argument against C-Rex is that it's ridiculous. That's it, that's the full width, breadth and depth of the argument against the C-Rex model. No facts, no proof, no science, no math, no indisputable knowledge or airtight logic, just the overwhelming unbelievability of the idea that there is no universe outside of consciousness.

It's very hard to believe. That's the only objection.

That's a real good thing to understand. Once you understand that, then you can understand how truth can be so unhidden, yet so unfound. It is the sheer unbelievability of C-Rex that protects it from detection. The flipside of this is the total believability of U-Rex, and the fact that everyone unreservedly agrees that U-Rex is reality.

Another real good thing to understand is that there is no such thing as a rational person. We are emotional creatures with some token capacity for reason. This isn't something we have to take on a case-by-case basis, it's absolutely true of absolutely everyone.

As I've said, nothing is being withheld from us. There is no agent or agency in charge of keeping us ignorant of our own nature. There is no conspiracy to keep us in the dark. It is our belief in the reality of reality that keeps us from noticing that it's a mirage. We are emotional beings, and emotion is the power of belief.

✧

As a trilogy-related aside, let me say that I hate mystery. I hate mystery so much that I went out and tracked it down and wherever I found it I killed it until I didn't find anymore. This is something I actually did, and at which I was perfectly successful. I destroyed shadows and darkness with light and clear-seeing. This is another way of expressing the awakening process, and the decisive question is, do you hate false-self more than you fear no-self? That's the battle; hatred of false self vs fear of no-self. This question can build up in you for years, and the exact moment that you take the First Step on the true journey of awakening is the exact moment that you answer this question. Picking up a six-inch knife and leaping into a bloody maelstrom to slay an unslayable beast doesn't mean you *have* answered this question, it *is* the answer.

✧

There are two things you can say about C-Rex: One, it's obviously not true. Two, it's irrefutably true.

So, there it is. Not only is the C-Rex model irrefutably true, it's infuriatingly irrefutably true. In response to Bishop Berkeley, Dr. Samuel Johnson refuted it thus: He kicked a rock and declared: "I refute it thus!"

That's what I think of as the Hissy Defense, like toppling a chessboard and declaring checkmate. I understand this reaction. People want to move forward and build themeparks of ideas and philosophies, and they don't want to be held back on a technicality, but that's really what we're looking at here – in paradigm terms, C-Rex is an extinction-level technicality. There is no universe out there, there is no proof, or even evidence, that there is, and anything that says otherwise is just a belief.

I said in one of the books that if professors of philosophy understood the cogito, they wouldn't be professors of philosophy. That's this, this is that. Kicking the rock is what everyone who sees it has to do because it's there and it's irrefutable. If you want to go into the amusement park and have a free ticket for every ride for the rest of your life, that's the price of admission; you have to kick the cogito and say "I refute it thus!" You can use more words to do it – Johnson was articulate in his succinctness – but the essence is the same. The only way to play in the park is to kick this rock and say, in whatever way works for you, "I refute it thus!"

Of course, most of us accomplish it through stupidity, zealotry or doublethink – the three-legged stool of delusion and all that – but anyone who wants to take an honest look at their circumstances must deal with the fact that nothing more than I-Am/Consciousness can ever be known.

❖

In the end the Party would announce that two and two made five, and you would have to believe it. It was inevitable that they should make that claim sooner or later: the logic of their position demanded it. Not merely the validity of experience, but the very existence of external reality, was tacitly denied by their philosophy. The heresy of heresies was common sense. And what was terrifying was not that they would kill you for thinking otherwise, but that they might be right. For, after all, how do we know that two and two make four? Or that the force of gravity works? Or that the past is unchangeable? If both the past and the external world exist only in the mind, and if the mind itself is controllable – what then?   -George Orwell, 1984

✤

The amount of reinforcement a model needs runs in inverse proportion to its structural integrity; a strong model needs little or no reinforcement, a weak model needs a lot. We don't need cathedrals and rituals and torture squads to convince us that the sun is a source of warmth and light, but if you want to go the other way and say the sun emits the cold and dark of night, then you're going to need alot of costumes and ceremonies and guys with hot pliers.

C-Rex is not as compelling as the warmth of the sun. In fact, you can't know C-Rex directly until you *un*know everything in the way of it. I can tell you that C-Rex is my living reality and it could be yours too, but it can't be yours the way that any given -ism can be yours, like some pre-packaged ideology you sign up for and slip into. Paradigm shifts are a little oversold and under-regulated these days. C-Rex is just a shiny plaything of the mind unless it's your living reality. Until then, it's just another quirky theory in a universe full of quirky theories.

Don't take all this too seriously. For one thing, it doesn't really matter. For another, time is on your side. You don't have to go out and sell this model to your PhD committee tomorrow. This stuff is far outside the comfort zones of the greatest minds your species has ever produced, and here you are making direct eye contact with it, so well done. Have fun, don't strain, enjoy the ride. Let the scientists and theologians and academics take all this theory-of-everything stuff seriously, you and I don't have to do that. We can be *seriously* serious; serious for our own purposes. We don't have to publish for peer review or worry about tenure and funding, all we have to do is go where honest inquiry leads. That's something we can do that the false agenda folks can't.

from

Song of Childhood

When the child was a child
It walked with its arms swinging,
wanted the brook to be a river,
the river to be a torrent,
and this puddle to be the sea.

When the child was a child,
it didn't know that it was a child,
everything was soulful,
and all souls were one.

When the child was a child,
it had no opinion about anything,
had no habits,
it often sat cross-legged,
took off running,
had a cowlick in its hair,
and made no faces when photographed.

When the child was a child,
it was the time for these questions:
Why am I me, and why not you?
Why am I here, and why not there?
When did time begin, and where does space end?
Is life under the sun not just a dream?
Is what I see and hear and smell
not just an illusion of a world before the world?
Given the facts of evil and people.
does evil really exist?
How can it be that I, who I am,
didn't exist before I came to be,
and that, someday, I, who I am,
will no longer be who I am?

It had visualized a clear image of Paradise,
 and now can at most guess,
 could not conceive of nothingness,
 and shudders today at the thought.

When the child was a child,
It was enough for it to eat an apple, bread,
And so it is even now.

When the child was a child,
Berries filled its hand as only berries do,
 and do even now,
Fresh walnuts made its tongue raw,
 and do even now,
 it had, on every mountaintop,
 the longing for a higher mountain yet,
 and in every city,
 the longing for an even greater city,
 and that is still so,
It reached for cherries in topmost branches of trees
 with an elation it still has today,
 has a shyness in front of strangers,
 and has that even now.
It awaited the first snow,
And waits that way even now.

When the child was a child,
It threw a stick like a lance against a tree,
And it quivers there still today.

Peter Handke

Theory & Practice

In theory there is no difference between
theory and practice. In practice there is.

Yogi Berra

FOR REASONS OF ACCURACY, I sometimes exchange the awkward term spiritual enlightenment for the awkwarder term truth-realization, and even the awkwardest term untruth-unrealization. The last is the least misleading because one does not *realize* truth. (You want truth? Consciousness is Truth and you are Consciousness. That's it. Congrats.) Rather, one undergoes the long self-peeling process of unknowing what is untrue – everything except I Am.

I draw this distinction because realization is the false promise many are making; that enlightenment, for instance, is a realization, and that all you have to do is listen and learn and perform practices and try really hard and be really patient and you will have this wonderful realization and be really enlightened. Realizations aren't the final destinations they're often promoted as, they're just another kind of belief, like a depiction of a place. If the place doesn't really exist, then a depiction is the best version of it, but if the place *does* really exist, then a depiction is the worst version of it. We settle for a depiction on the assumption that the place doesn't really exist, or that we can't really get there, but if the place is true, then it does and we can. And truth, it does not go without saying, is true. It's not a realization. It's the one thing that is not a belief.

A painting by René Magritte called *The Treachery of Images* shows a simple tobacco pipe and below it, in French, are the words, "This is not a pipe." It *is* a pipe, but it's not a pipe, it's a painting of a pipe, a depiction of a thing and not the thing itself. Similarly, a movie of a mountain is not a mountain, it's just a shifting pattern of light on a screen. I am on the stage, but I'm also out in the audience, and from that perspective, everything on the stage is the same, just as everything on a movie screen is light. Everything on the stage – you and me and table and chairs and time and space and all the rest – is just a shifting pattern of light on a screen. This is not a mystical revelation, it's just perception undistorted by layers of false belief.

Simulacra and Simulation, a 1981 essay by French philosopher Jean Baudrillard, describes what he calls the precession of simulacra. He describes the way we have moved away from the direct and authentic experience of reality, to a symbol-based simulation of reality in which the symbols have evolved through several generations until they no longer represent anything real, only prior abstractions. He's talking about developments in the last hundred years, but it's interesting to note that what he's saying in the micro is what we're saying in the macro; that the map has become the territory and has no underlying basis in reality.

Consciousness needs no depiction. Here you are, right now, right in the thick of it. What good is a theory of everything reduced to words or symbols compared to the direct experience of being? The only thing to realize is that the seeker is the sought. All there is is consciousness, and that thou art.

In the books, I talked about the First Step, and how that's where the actual journey of awakening begins. I borrowed Melville's example of a First Step; Ahab picking up a six-inch knife and hurling himself against a massive foe he couldn't possibly defeat, but could no longer stand to not hurl himself against. What Melville only hinted at was what led up to that First Step; what made a sane and respected sea captain go so insane that he arrived at a new and unsuspected kind of sanity. That's the period of long, slow compression where one explores every possible avenue and slowly discovers that there is nothing to be found. This is experienced as a shrinking of the world, a constriction of reality and self, and it tightens and tightens until it creates a pressure so unendurable that the First Step is taken involuntarily, spontaneously, irrevocably.

So that's a little bit about the real journey of awakening which I provide here to illustrate my point about the difference between theory and practice. Awakening isn't a theory, it's a journey. You don't arrive in C-Rex by convincing yourself that you're already there, but by destroying every shred of the illusion that you're not.

Meaning & Belief

Life has to be given a meaning because of the obvious
fact that it has no meaning.

Henry Miller

Life is without meaning. You bring the meaning to it.
The meaning of life is whatever you ascribe it to be.

Joseph Campbell

There is not one big cosmic meaning for all, there is
only the meaning we each give to our life, an individual
meaning, an individual plot, like an individual novel,
a book for each person.

Anais Nin

W HAT'S THE MEANING OF LIFE? That's like asking what's
the favorite color of life. Same as yours. What else?
The meaning of life is whatever yours means to you.

If you're not sure of the meaning of your life, look to your struggle, and to the causes and fruits of your struggle. Look to your strongest emotions; love, fear, hate. What do you want to create, preserve or destroy? What's the worst thing you could lose or the best thing you could gain? Maybe your meaning is the thing that most defines you, like an institution or an affliction. Your meaning might be as general as duty, or as specific as killing an enemy.

Maybe your meaning is to just keep plodding along, getting through the day. I'll guess that since you're reading this your fortunes aren't garbage-pickin' grim, but that doesn't mean you're not stuck in a dead-end life. (Though technically, I suppose we all are.)

Your meaning might not be visible to you now; maybe you don't see it yet and maybe you never will. It might not become apparent to you until you find yourself in a hospice or a burning car or falling from a building, and maybe never. Since there is no true meaning, being meaningless is at least being honest.

There is no objective meaning because there's no objective anything, there's only you and your subjective meaning. If, like me, you have a specific purpose or function, then that's your meaning. Maybe your whole life is leading up to a single act as simple as pressing a button, and that will resolve your whole life from random static to picture perfect.

Maybe you have a lot of meanings. Maybe last year the meaning of your life was the birth of a child and next year it will be the loss of a parent. Maybe love of child and fear of death are big, constant meanings and hungry and sleepy and horny are little, passing meanings.

Don't get too hung up on all this meaning of life business. It's a rabbit-hole issue that falsely posits the existence of meaning, life, and you. A more appropriate question to an I-Am/Consciousness entity would be, What is the meaning of consciousness?, and the only possible answer would be, Consciousness Is.

Maybe the meaning of your life is what your life means to you *now*. It's hard to understand that time doesn't exist because we have such a clear experience of past, present and future, but we don't really experience past and future, only present. Past and future are just ideas in the present. This means that there is only now, but what *is* now? We can't say what now *is* because there is no *not*-now. It's always now. There is only now. Now is.

Why would a sane person buy a gun and go to a mall and shoot a bunch of innocent people? Why would a sane person jump on a handgrenade to save his buddies? Both for the same reason, and it's the same reason their moms brought them into the world. They're all doing pretty much the same thing everyone is doing; struggling against the black hole within, demanding that their lives have meaning even if they have to kill or die to do it. But no-self is true self, no-meaning is true meaning, and no matter what you create, preserve or destroy, you can never put a dent in that.

We yearn for meaning, but since no-self is true self, the realization of one's perfect meaninglessness is the key to liberation. This is the realization that makes the First Step possible and begins the actual journey of awakening, but it's not really a realization and the First Step isn't an act of volition, it's the last square inch of false support disappearing from beneath your feet.

✧

Are you really just a tumbleweed of beliefs? That's how

selfhood seems from without, but from within it's not so simple. It appears that there are many influences and contributing factors that go into making you such a unique little snowflake; nature, nurture, karma, dharma, past lives, oversouls, infinite intelligence and more. Are these just beliefs, or are they the source of beliefs, or are they you-defining factors other than beliefs?

What's the difference between me and you? Between anyone and anyone else? Is it only belief that sets one being apart from another? In U-Rex, the answer is obviously no, but in C-Rex, it's obviously yes. That might seem absurd, but as the fog rolls out and the dream recedes, reality simply evaporates, leaving us alone in a desert landscape where the absurd becomes the obvious.

On the face of it, we are more than just the beliefs we've picked up along the way, but whatever makes us who we are is purely a U-Rex or X-Rex phenomenon. This is most clear in the most task-specific persons. If we speculate that there was a person named Mozart, and that this person was as history tells us, then we can reasonably conclude that he was more than the product of his nurturing, i.e., we can't swap baby Wolfie for just any kid off the street and expect him to also become a Mozart.

But of greater significance is what you can reasonably conclude about yourself. Regardless of what makes us who we are, no further truth lies in the direction of solving that mystery. The journey of self-discovery is not one of self-exploration but of self-annihilation. You must illuminate the shadowlands of your interior spaces and sever the tendrils of emotional energy that anchor you to selfhood and the dreamstate. There is no reconciling the irreconcilable, and apart from I Am, the only thing we can say for sure is that we can't say anything else for sure. It bears repeating; knowing what we cannot know is one of the most important things we can know, and except I Am, no conscious entity can ever know anything. Everything we know about who and what we are is false.

If you were to sit down and have a candid conversation with that aspect of yourself which is not intoxicated with wrong-knowing, you would be told that the person you think you are is no more closely related to what you really are than anyone else. Not only are you not you, you bear no resemblance to you and have no relationship to you. You could just as easily be anyone else, and maybe you are. In fact, you might be every*one* and every*thing* else. In fact, maybe you must be. This whole personal identity business unravels very quickly once you get a bit above it, and it doesn't unravel a little, it unravels completely.

The Veil of Perception

There's no reality except the one contained within us.
That's why so many people live an unreal life. They take
images outside them for reality and never allow the
world within them to assert itself.

Hermann Hesse

T HE MAJOR OBSTACLE TO ACCEPTING THE C-REX model is our clear and obvious perception that the world around us is real. How can it not be? I see it, touch it, hear it, taste and smell it. It's always there, always solid and stable. I experience it directly every waking minute of my life. It's just silly to say it doesn't exist, and that means that the C-Rex model is silly as well.

My response to that, as always, is revisit your assumptions. In this case, the assumption that we experience the world directly is false. No one has ever experienced this alleged world directly, and no one ever will. Weird, huh?

✧

"Spend more time with your hands," I suggest to Karl.

He stares at me blankly.

"Seriously, give your hands some serious thought. Make an effort to appreciate your hands; move them, observe them, feel they're actual connectedness to you."

Karl is studying his hands like he's never really seen them before. Or maybe he's messing with me, I can't read people.

Whenever I want to settle down and remind myself that I have this experience of a body in a spacetime energymatter amusement park, I study my hands. I do this many times a day. They remind me of where I am and how awesome it is, and that it can all change at any moment.

"As you appreciate your hands," I tell Karl, "reflect on the fact that you do not and cannot experience your hands directly."

He holds them up to show me, directly, and exhibits smug remorse at having defeated my foolish statement so easily.

"You don't experience your hands directly," I say. "The only thing you perceive directly is consciousness, so you experience the *perception* of your hands directly, but you experience your hands themselves, and your brain and beer and the past *in*directly."

"What's the difference between directly and indirectly?"

"The only thing you perceive directly is perception itself; consciousness."

"Like my hands."

"No, like your perception of your hands."

"But not my actual hands?"

"Not so actual, actually."

In philosophy this is called the Veil of Perception, meaning that all we really perceive is ideas of things, never the things themselves. My hands, for instance, are not experienced directly by me, but through sensory receptors that transmit electrochemical signals through a nervous system to a brain where they are interpreted and create the perception of hands, but, obviously, that whole sensory system, brain included, is just an idea. No matter how strongly I believe my hands and brain are real, they never rise above the level of non-probable possibility. This universe we experience can never be more than a belief. There's no proof, or even evidence, that physical reality is real. This is what it means to say that Maya's palace of delusion is constructed entirely of wisps of dreamstuff.

Brainwashed U-Rex cultmembers (you, I assume) believe in the existence of a physical universe *out there*, but no one has ever perceived it directly and no one ever will. Hence, the strange loop of consensus reality; we all agree that the universe is really out there, those agreeing with us being themselves out there.

Everything we experience through the senses is already second-hand at the moment of perception because the brain doesn't perceive anything, it just sits in its lightproof box and translates incoming sense-data into perceptions. Your alleged brain doesn't see, hear, taste or touch anything. You have no direct contact with a universe *out there*, only an internal movie, a projection on the screen of the mind. No one can ever perceive anything *out there* directly. That clear and obvious truth seems like something that scientists should preface every statement with, not bury, but if they don't bury it, it buries them. Their credibility might suffer if they have to begin every statement with "This is just baseless fiction masquerading as solid fact, of course, but..."

We are programmed from birth to suspend disbelief and let ourselves pretend reality is real, but if we want to stop pretending and find out what's *really* real, we have to reengage our critical disbelief systems and become rabidly, fanatically, pathologically skeptical. Philosophy calls it extreme skepticism. I call it distinguishing the known from the believed, which doesn't seem that extreme to me. You have to draw a line somewhere, and between belief and knowledge seems like a good place to do it.

I can assert that I live in the 21st century, but that's just a belief based on rumor and hearsay, or it could be the lingering effects of last night's 34th century audience participation hypnosis event which I was instructed to forget I attended, or the setting of an in-flight period-piece sense-movie being piped into my cryogenically suspended brain during extended space travel, or any of countless other scenarios. How can I be sure? The same way I can be sure of anything – I can't.

It might seem at first that C-Rex isn't possible because our reality is just too real to be a dreamlike phenomenon, but when we start looking at what we really know and how we know and the nature of knowing, then the unreality of reality is revealed. We are only conscious of consciousness. That's a powerful reminder of what cannot be accepted as real. I am not aware of my hands, rather, the three – I, awareness and hands – are one; perceiver-perception-perceived. Consciousness.

✧

We develop our sense of object permanence by the age of two, but we might still wonder if something really exists when we no longer observe it. We outgrow such questions, but not because we answered them. It's perfectly valid to ask; How do I know my bicycle really exists when I don't see it? The answer is; I don't. The better question is; How do I know my bicycle exists when I *do* see it? The answer is; I don't. The best question is; Then how the hell do I know *any*thing exists? The answer is; I don't.

Is something true when I am conscious of it? No. Consciousness is true, but the content of consciousness is not. I can never perceive the external world directly, but I do perceive perception directly. My perception of a cheeseburger does not prove the existence of an actual cheeseburger, but the perception itself is perfectly real and valid – to me. The cheeseburger is as real as it seems. Strength of perception varies, so the sight, smell, taste and feel of any given cheeseburger in hand is more real than any given cheeseburger in imagination, but both cheeseburgers are just perceptions – one more real, but neither more true.

✧

"Perception is perception," I say to Karl, "it doesn't have to be qualified because it is what it is. My perception of a cheeseburger and my perception of the stars are equally valid. However, if I extrapolate from those perceptions to declare that I have a physical body in a timespace energymatter universe full of cheeseburgers and stars, then I have wandered off into baseless speculation by trying to weave a physical universe from wisps of dreamstuff."

"Which everyone does," he says.

"Sure, which everyone does, if there really is an everyone, instead of just a lot of wispy dreamstuff."

"Ah, yes," says the wispy dreamstuff I call Karl, "of

course."

"But," continues the wispy dreamstuff I call me, "if I don't try to extrapolate a physical universe based on my perceptions, then there is no conflict. My cheeseburger generates sensory awareness, which is a reality in the perceptual tripartite of my being, so when that perception exists, it is a part of me, of my me-ness and now-ness."

"So if the universe isn't real," asks Karl, examining his hands, "then where does it come from?"

"As real as it is to you is as real as it is," I say with a vague sense of self-plagiarization. Then I realize that I need to say that same thing using only two-letter words. "As, uh, *is* as it is to, er, *me,* is as is as it is," I say triumphantly.

"Huh?" says Karl, using three letters.

"Never mind," I say. "Paradigm-hopping is a tricky business. There are a lot of ramifications of C-Rex that are very difficult to process theoretically. It's easy to say that consciousness is not within time and space, but to really understand it, you have to relax out of all your time-hardened, emotionally empowered beliefs that tell you otherwise. You don't need any new beliefs, but you will begin to see how entrenched and inflexible your old ones really are. There is no time or space, there is only consciousness. There is no before or after, no here or there, there is only is. So, to answer your question, the universe comes from consciousness and consciousness is."

"And that answer satisfies you?"

"Perfectly. I've called C-Rex home for more than twenty years and I understand the things I'm saying directly, not based on weak intermediaries like words or concepts or beliefs. I see everything forever in all directions. I see no mystery or possibility of mystery anywhere, and I see that there's no place for mystery to hide. I hope I'm conveying something of the simplicity and obviousness of all this. Trying to express the inexpressible is a fool's errand, but I've never let that stop me."

This is simple stuff and to get it you gotta get simple. Believing or disbelieving C-Rex is irrelevant. If C-Rex is not your state of reality, then it's just another concept-toy you can play with and forget, but you've come this far, so why not take it for a spin? Treat it like a lens and reassess your world through it. See how everything resolves into clarity. Look around. Look at everything and everyone. Look at any mystery, ask any question. Look at what you're most sure of – your hands, your brain, a cheeseburger – and ask how you know they're real. The answer is, you never do.

Speculation & Make-Believe

Do not keep saying to yourself, if you can possibly avoid it,
"But how can it be like that?" because you will get "down
the drain," into a blind alley from which nobody has yet
escaped. Nobody knows how it can be like that.

Richard P. Feynman

S O NOW THAT WE KNOW what can and can't be known as
true, we can take a look at that which can't be known,
but which we might as well believe anyway. This is back
down the rabbit-hole, where the mountain is a mountain
again, and where everything is real but nothing is true. The
trick is drawing a distinct line between real and true. We
can't accept anything as true except I-Am/Consciousness, but
whatever we believe is real, is real.

To re-enter the amusement park is to re-suspend disbelief; to accept the *virtual* reality of the dreamstate as *real* reality. For instance, I like to pretend that I'm sane and that I have free will. Might as well, right? I also pretend that I am my character, that my memories are trustworthy, and that time and space and the world are as they seem. Kinda gotta.

And frankly, why not? I have no belief to uphold, no teaching to adhere to, no one to convince of anything. I'm done. *Done* done. I don't have to act or dress or behave a certain way. Yes, I have this overlighting co-creative intelligence thing, but that's just another belief, like pretending I'm sane.

With all that said, we can take a closer look at some speculations within C-Rex that we might as well accept as real, like filling ballast tanks with dead-weight in order to submerge.

❖

As stated, one of the main things I make-believe is true is the overlighting intelligence with which I align myself. I speculate that I am in a co-creative relationship with an intelligence and will infinitely superior to my own. I observe that I exist within energetic patterns that flow like currents. I observe that when I act in alignment with these subtle energetic currents, all goes well, desires manifest, direction is clear, ease and smoothness are natural. I observe that I have developed a high degree of sensitivity to this energy, and that I'm able to make micro-corrections before any significant non-smoothness occurs.

Perfect intelligence is easy for me to believe. It almost proves out logically, I perceive it without the senses, and it is so nearly certain to me that I'd almost claim it as truth, which I would never say about anything else. Sure, it's all speculation, but I might as well speculate that I'm sane, and if I *am* sane, then perfect intelligence is my operating system. PIos.

My character is something else I go along with. What's an actor without a character to play? No-self is true self, but actors on a stage need personas and costumes and backstories, and I already have all that, so that's how I roll. The mountain is a mountain again. What else would I do, walk around as no-self? Not an option. There is no such thing as an enlightened person in the dreamstate because you can't be true in a false context, or unlimited in a limited context. Conversely, truth is uninhabitable. No one lives where the mountain isn't a mountain, no one resides outside of the dreamstate. You're either in Maya's Palace of Delusion, or you're nowhere.

I also treat the wysiwyg universe as real. This is the dreamstate reality I find myself in and, except for not existing, I don't find it objectionable. For that reason, and because it would be damned inconvenient not to, I accept apparent reality at face value. I said in the first book that I believe everything indiscriminately, and this is that. Being awake in the dreamstate, I don't need to worry about discriminating between what's real and what's not. Everything in a dream is equally real, so what is there to discriminate about?

The apparent world, starting with my apparent brain and working outward, is easy to believe, and is a necessary convention of life in the dreamstate. The wysiwyg universe is where I live, this is where my mountain is a mountain again. I call it home, but I never confuse it with truth. I may inhabit the dreamstate, but I never slip back into non-lucidity.

✧

So far we haven't stretched this suspended disbelief stuff

too far. It's all been mainly environmental and centered on my direct experience, but now we have to consider a very big leap: You-Are/Consciousness. Do I believe in you?

If I don't make-believe that other conscious entities exist, then I am the only inhabitant of creation; the sole beholder. In this light, I-Am/Consciousness is all, and what I *know* to be true is all that *is* true. This is the enlightened perspective, the alpha and omega of knowledge, the whole of knowable truth, and anything more than this is baseless speculation. That's the bottom line.

But when I duck back down the rabbit-hole and into the amusement park of mixed metaphors and infinite possibilities, I can passively grant the existence of innumerable other I-Am/Entities. To do so is to speculate that every I-Am/Entity is the center of their own dreamstate universe, just as I am of mine. So now I'm speculating that there are innumerable discrete consciousness entities like myself, and each one experiences its own universe, resulting in infinite unconnected universes; the Multiverse.

Which is just how it appears, almost. It actually appears that, yes, there are many of us, but that furthermore, we are all sharing a dreamspace. That's how it looks in U-Rex, right? Like there's one reality and we're all in it together? The universe is the infinite sheet of paper and we're just a bunch of little specks of consciousness that appear and disappear.

Well, what seems so obvious in U-Rex is wildly speculative in C-Rex. Even having granted the You-Are Multiverse in which you and innumerable others are self-aware entities like myself, it's still a far cry from granting that we share a Matrix-like reality. When we speculate this, we are speculating innumerable discreet consciousnesses operating in parallel in a shared timespace environment; parallel universes.

The difference between multiverse and parallel universes, as we're retasking these terms, is like the difference between a single-player or multiplayer environment in a video game. A multiverse scenario is like single-player gameplay where millions of other people might be playing in the same virtual environment, but they are all completely separate and apart with no overlap or shared influence. Nothing that happens in my single-player universe has any effect in yours or any other. I nuke my Paris, your Paris is fine. A parallel universe scenario is like multiplayer gameplay where there is a single environment experienced by two or more entities from differing perspectives. I nuke my Paris, everyone's Paris is nuked.

Karl and I sit outside drinking good beer and looking up at the stars. In C-Rex, Karl, beer and stars are just elements in my dreamstate. When I speculate a multiverse, then Karl is still an element in my dream, but I grant the possibility of an actual Karl somewhere in consciousness, possibly sitting next to a facsimile of me and looking up at similar stars, possibly not. When I speculate a parallel universe, then Karl and I are sharing a virtual environment in consciousness, perceiving the same stars from different perspectives. That last scenario, Karl's and my universes operating apart but in parallel – Parallel Universes – is the most obvious and least likely.

As amusing as it may be to speculate, we cannot spin stable and comprehensive theories of everything out of thin air. I know of one perfect theory of everything, and I know there is no other. Truth is the only possible theory of everything, and trying to understand anything beyond I-Am/Consciousness could never be more than virtual gameplay.

From *The Restaurant at the
End of the Universe* by Douglas Adams

...and his eyes, though open, seemed closed.

THE RAIN PELTED AND DANCED on the corrugated iron roof of the small shack that stood in the middle of this patch of scrubby land. The noise of the rain on the roof of the shack was deafening within, but went largely unnoticed by its occupant, whose attention was otherwise engaged. He was a tall shambling man with rough straw-coloured hair that was damp from the leaking roof. His clothes were shabby, his back was hunched, and his eyes, though open, seemed closed.

In his shack was an old beaten-up armchair, an old scratched table, an old mattress, some cushions and a stove that was small but warm. He stood up and found a glass that was lying on the floor by the mattress. He poured in a measure from his whisky bottle. He sat again.

"Perhaps some other people are coming to see me," he said.

The door opened.

"Hello?" said the man.

"Ah, excuse me," said Zarniwoop, "I have reason to believe..."

"Do you rule the Universe?" said Zaphod.

The man smiled at him.

"I try not to," he said. "Are you wet?"

Zaphod looked at him in astonishment.

"Wet?" he cried. "Doesn't it look as if we're wet?"

"That's how it looks to me," said the man, "but how you feel about it might be an altogether different matter. If you feel warmth makes you dry, you'd better come in."

They went in.

They looked around the tiny shack, Zarniwoop with slight distaste, Trillian with interest, Zaphod with delight.

"Hey, er..." said Zaphod, "what's your name?"

The man looked at them doubtfully.

"I don't know. Why, do you think I should have one? It seems very odd to give a bundle of vague sensory perceptions a name."

He invited Trillian to sit in the chair. He sat on the edge of the chair, Zarniwoop leaned stiffly against the table and Zaphod lay on the mattress.

"Wowee!" said Zaphod, "the seat of power!" He tickled the cat.

"Listen," said Zarniwoop, "I must ask you some questions."

"Alright," said the man kindly, "you can sing to my cat if you like."

"Would he like that?" asked Zaphod.

"You'd better ask him," said the man.

"Does he talk?" said Zaphod.

"I have no memory of him talking," said the man, "but I am very unreliable."

Zarniwoop pulled some notes out of a pocket.

"Now," he said, "you do rule the Universe, do you?"

"How can I tell?" said the man.

Zarniwoop ticked off a note on the paper.

"How long have you been doing this?"

"Ah," said the man, "this is a question about the past, is it?"

Zarniwoop looked at him in puzzlement. This wasn't exactly what he had been expecting.

"Yes," he said.

"How can I tell," said the man, "that the past isn't a fiction designed to account for the discrepancy between my immediate physical sensations and my state of mind?"

"No, listen to me," said Zarniwoop, "people come to you do they? In ships…"

"I think so," said the man. He handed the bottle to Trillian.

"And they ask you," said Zarniwoop, "to make decisions for them? About people's lives, about worlds, about economies, about wars, about everything going on out there in the Universe?"

"Out there?" said the man, "out where?"

"Out there!" said Zarniwoop pointing at the door.

161

"How can you tell there's anything out there," said the man politely, "the door's closed."

"But you know there's a whole Universe out there!" cried Zarniwoop. "You can't dodge your responsibilities by saying they don't exist!"

The ruler of the Universe thought for a long while whilst Zarniwoop quivered with anger.

"You're very sure of your facts," he said at last, "I couldn't trust the thinking of a man who takes the Universe – if there is one – for granted."

Zarniwoop still quivered, but was silent.

"I only decide about my Universe," continued the man quietly. "My Universe is my eyes and my ears. Anything else is hearsay."

"But don't you believe in anything?"

The man shrugged and picked up his cat.

"I don't understand what you mean," he said.

"You don't understand that what you decide in this shack of yours affects the lives and fates of millions of people? This is all monstrously wrong!"

"I don't know. I've never met all these people you speak of. And neither, I suspect, have you. They only exist in words we hear. It is folly to say you know what is happening to other people. Only they know, if they exist. They have their own Universes of their own eyes and ears."

"Do you believe other people exist?" insisted Zarniwoop.

"I have no opinion. How can I say?"

Zarniwoop continued.

"But don't you understand that people live or die on your word?"

"It's nothing to do with me," he said, "I am not involved with people. The Lord knows I am not a cruel man."

"Ah!" barked Zarniwoop, "you say 'The Lord'. You believe in something!"

"My cat," said the man benignly, picking it up and stroking it, "I call him The Lord. I am kind to him."

"Alright," said Zarniwoop, pressing home his point, "How do you know he exists? How do you know he knows you to be kind, or enjoys what he thinks of as your kindness?"

"I don't," said the man with a smile, "I have no idea. It merely pleases me to behave in a certain way to what appears to be a cat. Do you behave any differently? Please, I think I am tired."

Zarniwoop heaved a thoroughly dissatisfied sigh and looked about.

"Where are the other two?" he said suddenly.

"What other two?" said the ruler of the Universe, settling back into his chair and refilling his whisky glass.

"Beeblebrox and the girl! The two who were here!"

"I remember no one. The past is a fiction to account for..."

"Stuff it," snapped Zarniwoop and ran out into the rain.

The Truman Show

We accept the reality of the world
with which we are presented.

"Christof"

I MENTIONED THE MOVIE *The Truman Show* to the twins on several occasions, but they had never seen it. Actually, I hadn't seen it since it was first released, so on my last night with them we rented it and watched together. Karl and Sandy joined us, so it turned into family movie night, plus one. Cozy.

The movie is a basic parable of the journey of awakening from delusion. At the end of his journey, Truman Burbank escapes through the final door into freedom from the artificial environment – Seahaven – in which he was raised. He steps through the door into a broader reality that is essentially the same world he's always known, but on a larger scale; same paradigm, same dynamics, same everything really, just one level up. Just like Neo in *The Matrix*, Truman doesn't escape from Maya, he just leaps from one turtle to the next.

"So, pretend it's you opening that door," I tell John and Claire after the movie when they come to discuss it with me. "Your whole life has been moving toward this; you've undergone crisis after crisis, fought battle after battle, destroyed illusion after illusion. You've been living in a state of unrelenting emotional upheaval as your world collapsed around you, you've made a great journey, and now you're about to discover the truth of your being. You're about to leave the only reality you've ever known and step into a new, bigger reality you've never seen and only recently began to suspect. Okay?"

"Okay," they agree in unison.

"Okay. In the movie-metaphor, Truman is just stepping out of a microcosm into the regular cosm we all know; it's really the same paradigm he's known in the vast soundstage of Seahaven, but on a different scale. He's just tunneling from one cell into a larger cell, right?"

I wait for their reply because this is a good time to have everyone on the same page. They assure me they are.

"But what if, instead of standing at a door to the next level, he was standing at the *final* door? A door that wouldn't open into just another layer, but beyond *all* layers and into the ultimate, eternal and infinite reality. What if he'd killed his final Buddha, took his final bow, and stepped through that door into the perfect void of nothing forever? What then?"

They treat the question as rhetorical and stare at me.

"There's no time or space on the other side of that final door," I continue, "no energy or matter, no motion, no relativeness, no otherness. The mountain is not a mountain. There are no people or places out there, no character to play or audience to play to; it's all truth and no Truman. There's nothing to perceive, so there's no perception, and without perceived and perception, how can there be a perceiver?"

"What does that mean?" asks Claire.

"Nothing forever," I say. "The void of undifferentiated consciousness."

"But what does that *mean?*" asks John.

"It doesn't *mean* anything," I say, "it just is."

They look at each other, and back at me.

⁕

Let's say Truman makes it to that final door. Then what? Maybe he extends his hand through the door and sees it disappear, or maybe he dives out and lands back on the spot he dove from, or maybe... well, we kind of run out of metaphors at this point. Standing at that final door isn't *like* anything. It's the end of the line. The final question is destroyed, the final veil is drawn back, the final gate is opened. Everything is understood. Perfect knowledge is attained because all false knowledge has been destroyed. He has arrived at the only place in Maya's universe where there is no further, a strange and lonely place called Done. All he can do now is turn around and re-enter the false reality he gave everything to escape. Only now he is, quite literally, disillusioned.

And there it is. The enlightened guy is really just a bad sport who stomped off in a black rage and then slinks back after discovering that there's nowhere else to go. I called enlightenment a booby prize, and this is why, but truth-realization isn't achieved by desire, so it's only those who can't get there that would be disappointed. The black rage guy didn't want to become something true, he wanted to *un*become something false. That *is* achievable, and that's the only way it works.

✧

In the movie, the last thing Truman does before going through that door is kill the Buddha. He kills God; *his* God. He's "killed" everyone else, destroyed every other lie and delusion, and only this last barrier remains. For Truman, it's Christof, his creator/director/producer. For anyone, killing that final whatever and opening that final door are two ways of saying the same thing – Done.

Note that Truman did not make a spiritual journey. He wasn't a practitioner of any technique or follower of any path, he had no teacher or lineage, he was simply someone who detected a loose thread in the fabric of his reality and began tugging on it, and had the purity of intent necessary to keep on tugging, even though the thing he was unraveling was himself.

✧

After you make the great journey – a journey of surmounting obstacles and confronting fears, of unmasking deceivers, of burning everything, of arriving at that final gate and killing that final Buddha, of beholding the infinite truth directly – after all that, then what?

Then done. Then you pull the door shut and leave all that truth-void shit out there where it belongs. Then you know. Then you understand. Then the houselights are thrown on and the whole tragicomic farce is revealed, and you'll never be able to really suspend disbelief again. Then the artificial environment you went to such lengths to get out of would be looking pretty sweet, and escape would be looking pretty dumb, like breaking out of a submarine or a spaceship.

Movie Truman steps through the door and leaves his Seahaven behind, but our oxymoronic true-man doesn't go through the door. He can't, there's no such thing as *him* anywhere else. He's discovered that he's a prisoner in protective custody, a holodeck character who can't exist outside of his holographic environment. He's still on the stage, but now the illusion has been shattered; no more meaning, nothing left to do, just a whole lot of whatever.

For me, after about ten years of acclimating myself to what was now effectively a lifeless desert-planet, a larger pattern was revealed and I was able to relax into it. That allowed the creation of the books, which has been an amusing and engaging pastime for which I am grateful.

So, in the movie, Truman passes through the door and the credits roll, but in our final-door version, he does not go out. He turns around and goes back in.

What is this new person that returns from that final door back into the vast soundstage of Seahaven? Is he magically endowed? Is he a mystic? Does he have special powers? Can he grant boons? Does he return in the boat, or can he walk on water? If a non-awake resident of Seahaven looks at our Truman, will they see in him the highest human ideal, or just some misfit who doesn't seem to belong? There is nothing different in his appearance; he doesn't glow or levitate or radiate benevolence, he doesn't spew wisdom or have a sagely answer to every question, he doesn't know any shortcuts to that final door, or why anyone would want to get there. He is, as Layman P'ang said, neither holy nor wise, just an ordinary fellow who has completed his work.

What a true Truman returns to find is a Seahaven full of actors. What he once saw as people like himself are now something else; something bewildering and unrelatable. One thing he knows is that they don't know what he knows. They haven't undergone those personal unravelings and stood at that final door. They haven't made the ultimate journey from which return itself is an illusion.

They don't know where they are.

So what, at most, are they? Children, straw dogs, zombies. None of them, to our true-man's clear new eyes, better or worse than another. Not bad, not good, just asleep at most and non-sentient apparitions at least. They are set design, props, extras. He is no longer one of them or related to them, and never will be again.

Movie Truman walks out of Seahaven into a new life of love and freedom, but our true-man is now consigned to walk alone in a world that he knows is not real, cloaked in a body and persona to which he feels no connection, surrounded by actors playing a pointless drama. He has traded everything for nothing, and made a good deal.

The Enlightened Perspective

Give a man a match and he'll be warm for a night.
Set a man on fire and he'll be warm for the rest of
his life.

C ONVINCED? YOU SHOULDN'T BE. How could you be?
At most, you could accept the C-Rex model enough
to muddle your current model. Maybe you can appreciate
C-Rex conceptually and use it as a tool to re-evaluate existing
beliefs. Maybe it's a slow-burn thing, and now that you've
been exposed, you'll find it seeping into your worldview in
the months and years to come. I'm just guessing. No one
could actually transition into C-Rex except by transitioning
out of U-Rex, but maybe this glimpse could nudge you
toward a more belief-defying life.

Speaking of which, I'm a perfect example of someone who is living a belief-defying life. I live on a planet where a hundred billion people live or have lived, and though I am unstellar in all respects, I'm supposed to believe that out of countless millions and billions of people who are vastly more intelligent, courageous and heartfelt than myself, I am one of very few to achieve true spiritual enlightenment.

I mean, c'mon, *seriously*?

Who could believe such a contrived fantasy? I'm certainly not that gullible, but it's my life so what can I do? I could try to escape, but I did all the escaping I could and this is where it got me. It's as if you plugged a little old lady into the mind machine in *Total Recall* instead of Arnold, and now she believes she's an interplanetary superspy kicking ass and saving worlds. It doesn't fit, it can't be reconciled, it's just too outlandish. A big, muscular guy like Arnold, yeah, sure, maybe he can't tell if it's live or Memorex, but a little old lady should know the difference, and so should I.

No wonder I think the universe is a big playful puppy. Yeah, maybe I'll get ass cancer tomorrow and decide the universe is a rabid fuckin' pitbull, but for now I'm just going with the flow and playing this unlikely role. Life is but a dream, so why quibble? I get to dream that I'm an enlightened spiritual guy who writes books and digs dogs and swings in hammocks – why rock *that* boat?

❖

The definition of consciousness we're using here – perceiver-perception-perceived – qualifies as Atmanic Consciousness, but what can we say about Brahmanic Consciousness? We can say that Brahmanic Consciousness is truth, is infinite, is the ground of Atmanic Consciousness, which is all correct, but which doesn't really *say* anything. Consciousness is. We can't say more than that. Because Brahmanic Consciousness is infinite and without attribute, we can only say what it's not, not what it is. Unsatisfying, right? I know, but I don't make the rules, and this one can't be broken. Everyone tries to break it, of course, by ascribing attributes to Brahman/Truth/God/Consciousness, but when you take all attributes away, you are left with the infinite otherlessness that we are calling Brahmanic Consciousness.

Admitting that we don't and can't understand Brahmanic Consciousness isn't meant to suggest that we do understand Atmanic Consciousness. The latter is the one we experience and which seems certain, while the former seems like dry theory, but in truth, we can be sure Brahmanic Consciousness does exist and that Atmanic Consciousness doesn't. Now *that's* a paradox.

There is only truth. Untruth does not exist. That's why untruth-unrealization is the more accurate term, and why there's no such thing as an enlightened being. In truth, there is no perceiver, perception or perceived. There's no this/not-that, no here/not-there, no now/not-then, no me/not you. There is only the otherless, attributeless, infinite *is*.

Can we say that Brahman/Truth/God/Consciousness is fractal and/or holographic? Sure, why not. But wouldn't that be an attribute? No, it's just a way of describing the infinite to say that as much as you zoom in or out, you can always zoom further in or out, so that any part is the equal of the whole. If that's what we mean by fractal or holographic, fine, but is it significant? Only insofar as your I Am-ness makes you a part of the whole, and therefore, the *whole* whole.

Let's go back to that sheet of white paper which extends in all directions forever. Now let's erase all the dots and circles.

What's left? Perfect, unblemished nothing forever. No divisions or distinctions, no ends or beginnings, no borders or edges. We have arrived at truth, but who has arrived? No one, of course. Not true self, but no-self. There is no part, only the whole. You were never a dot, you were always the sheet. To be anything is to be everything. It cannot be otherwise and cannot be simplified further. Brahman is Atman, Atman is Brahman. That thou art.

❖

All this wordiness completely fails to depict what I experience as the living reality of C-Rex. That's the dissatisfying nature of this document for me; it's an amusing challenge to try to express all this stuff in some way that someone might find interesting, but when I read through it, there's no sense of the clean, simple, unmysterious reality that I experience. Having undergone the process of untruth-unrealization, I am left *not* in an elevated state of superior knowledge, but in a knowledgeless state of superior elevation. I see everything, I understand everything, I know nothing.

Does perfect intelligence exist? I vote yes, but that's what I think, not what I know. Yes, I perceive perfect intelligence, but I perceive all sorts of crazy shit. In my mountain-again rabbit-hole, I perceive overlighting intelligence and I operate in alignment with it. I may not understand it, and I could be wrong, but for more than twenty years now this has been my sole mode of navigation, and it has been not just constant and unerring, but magical. For me, perfect intelligence is synonymous with consciousness, so this co-creative, higher-knowing relationship I experience is more than my *connection* with Godmind, it's my Godmind*ness*.

❖

We all draw a line between what we believe and what we don't. This line is different for everyone and can move around a lot in the course of a lifetime. All we're doing here is drawing a line between what we *know* and what we don't. This line is exactly the same for everyone, and it can never move for anyone. On the known side is I-Am/Consciousness, and on the other side is everything else. This line, between knowledge and belief, is the one and only bottom line of being. If you know this directly, then you reside in C-Rex. If you *don't* know this directly, then you reside in – wait for it – C-Rex. You only *believe* you're in U-Rex.

There are plenty of people making the same basic case of IAM – Idealistic Antimaterialistic Monism – that we're making here. I could have easily doubled or tripled the size of this document by citing past and present proponents of this and similar models, but as I said, less is definitely more. You can go find all that stuff if you're interested, but the whole argument is as simple as we said in the first chapter: *If,* truth is all, *and,* consciousness exists, *then,* consciousness is all. It's not a belief thing, it's a see-for-yourself thing, and it's sitting in plain sight. We don't need a hundred experts to tell us what's right behind us, we just need to turn around and look.

Convinced? You can't be. As we sit and watch the world, and experience it in all its diversity and complexity, its realness is undeniable and the idea that it's all just a dream is obviously nonsense. I agree. Everyone agrees. Time and space, energy and matter, causality and duality; all indisputably real, just not true. If you want to understand this for yourself, you must first realize that you're on your own, that you have no teachers or teaching to aid you, no friends or fellowship to comfort you. You must sort this out for yourself because your self is the thing to be sorted. The great mystery isn't a problem of logic to be solved, but a thousand-headed hydra of emotion to be slain. We can call that hydra Maya, but it's really you.

But why bother? Leave truth to those who can't leave it alone. It's literally nothing, a singularly pointless achievement. Who wants to be the only sober adult at a party of punchdrunk revelers? Everyone is shitfaced on false-knowledge – gods and prophets, seers and sages, philosophers and scientists, kings and queens, your parents and teachers, everyone you ever knew or looked up to or prayed to – all of them completely besotted with belief, and why the hell not? An amusement park is no place for sobriety. The dreamstate is no place for lucidity. Truth is irrelevant.

What's *not* irrelevant is shaking off our self-imposed puniness and expanding into our full and rightful potential; Human Adulthood. That's where everything begins. Whether it's getting there or going beyond, there is no other thing to do or way to go. Human Adulthood is the key to everything, and if you're on the wrong side of it, nothing else matters. Human Adulthood is the thing you should pray for and fight for, the thing you should quit your job, abandon your family, and risk your life for. There's serious work to be done, and maybe you're reading this because that's the thing you want to know; that there really *is* something unbelievably awesome to be achieved, and you really *can* achieve it. And if it takes religion or a twelve-step program or prison or a broken neck to get you there, then those things are a hell of a lot more valuable to you than any book could ever be.

Forget all the spiritual malarkey. We have our hands full just becoming who and what we really are, and overcoming the all-pervading fear that subverts this natural process.

Adulthood is not a lofty spiritual attainment, it's just normal development unravaged by the epidemic of fear. It's the death of the flesh and birth of the spirit, and in a well-adjusted society we'd all go through it at puberty. It's not spiritual or religious or philosophical or scientific; it's just our natural development uncorrupted, and getting there isn't the end, it's just the beginning.

Human Adulthood is the one clear and universal course-heading; to, through and beyond, discovering who you really are and what the amusement park really is, and, most importantly, that there's no difference between the two. The real point of understanding the C-Rex paradigm is not to get there, but to realize that you've never been anywhere else. *You* are the journey and *you* are the destination, and when you really understand that, you'll understand that you didn't just finish reading this book, you just finished writing it.

The Last Religion

The name of God is Truth.

Hindu proverb

the only
True Church
is the
Church of Truth

ALETHEOLOGY
(Aletheia = Truth) (Theos = God) (-logy = Study of)

"The Study of God-Truth"
Mind is Church ~ Thought is Prayer ~ Truth is God
No amount of skepticism could ever be too extreme.

*For True thou art,
and to Truth thou shalt return.*

THE TEN SUGGESTIONS
Think

Believe Nothing

Doubt Everything

Fly to Fear

Get Real

Hate thy Ego

Love thy Death

Kill all Buddhas

Burn it All

Further

vitam impendere vero
Stake Life Upon Truth

Welcome.

Also by Jed McKenna

THE ENLIGHTENMENT TRILOGY

SPIRITUAL ENLIGHTENMENT
THE DAMNEDEST THING

SPIRITUALLY INCORRECT ENLIGHTENMENT

SPIRITUAL WARFARE

WWW.WISEFOOLPRESS.COM

CPSIA information can be obtained at www.ICGtesting.com
Printed in the USA
BVOW08s1340030813

327618BV00005B/19/P